"*The Bible Unwrapped* bears untold gifts, as rich and valuable in their own way as those brought to a child by wise ones two thousand years ago. Reading Scripture is the key to reading life that stands at the heart of following Jesus. Do not let this unique gift pass by unopened and unenjoyed."

—**LEONARD SWEET**, bestselling author, scholar, and speaker

"You need this book in your church, and in your work with people who are searching for answers. It is the missing piece for our discussions on current topics and the Bible."

—**DOTTIE ESCOBEDO-FRANK**, pastor, author, and speaker

"The book you are about to read is a rare treasure. I have read countless books that introduce readers to the Bible. I can honestly say that I have found none as enjoyable to read—without sacrificing anything by way of biblical scholarship—as this one."

—**GREGORY A. BOYD**, senior pastor of Woodland Hills Church, from foreword

"I believe in the authoritative, infallible, inerrant Word of God—and his name is Jesus. As someone who wants to know Jesus, I treasure the Bible as the place I can go to have a supernatural rendezvous with the living Christ. I'm so very thankful for this book by Meghan Larissa Good! *The Bible Unwrapped* is a book about the Book that will lead you to the person who will change your life."

—**BRUXY CAVEY**, author of *Reunion* and senior pastor of The Meetinghouse

"*The Bible Unwrapped* makes an invaluable contribution to the literature that seeks to explain the Bible. It invites readers to see the Bible for what it is: a collection of sacred texts through which God has spoken and continues to speak."

—**SAFWAT MARZOUK**, associate professor of Old Testament and Hebrew Bible at Anabaptist Mennonite Biblical Seminary

"In an age when the Bible is increasingly suspect, *The Bible Unwrapped* offers hope for followers of Jesus who are perplexed by the various issues that arise as they engage our sacred library of texts. Well written, poetic at times, hilarious at other times, and deeply informed by solid scholarship, this is a resource for anyone wanting to take another step forward in their faith journey. This book about the Book is a gift to the church!"

—**KURT WILLEMS**, writer, podcaster, and lead pastor at Pangea Church

"What the Bible is all about is best captured by this scholar-preacher's powerful words: 'a relationship, a dialogue, a dynamic dance between God and humans, responding to each other's movements.' Meghan Larissa Good's heart and mind combine in a very special talent that will entice readers into this dance."

—**PAUL BORGMAN**, author of *David, Saul, and God* and *Written to Be Heard*

"For all its popularity, the Bible is often misunderstood. Meghan Larissa Good skillfully reminds us that the messy and sacred world of the Bible is not a how-to book for life but a window through which we can view God's story and encounter the living Christ."

—**DEREK HOGAN**, assistant professor of New Testament at Campbell Divinity School

"Filled with humor, learned footnotes, and an abiding faith, *The Bible Unwrapped* is an accessible primer on Scripture and interpretation for college students and parishioners alike. Good delivers excellence, treating the difficulties of the Bible head-on while commending its witness as God-breathed revelation, always with an eye toward application."

—**JOHN T. NOBLE**, associate professor of Bible and religion at Huntington University

THE BIBLE
UNWRAPPED

THE BIBLE UNWRAPPED

MAKING SENSE OF SCRIPTURE TODAY

MEGHAN LARISSA GOOD

FOREWORD BY GREGORY A. BOYD

HERALD PRESS

Harrisonburg, Virginia

Herald Press
PO Box 866, Harrisonburg, Virginia 22803
www.HeraldPress.com

Library of Congress Cataloging-in-Publication Data
Names: Good, Meghan Larissa, author.
Title: The Bible unwrapped : making sense of scripture today / Meghan Larissa
   Good.
Description: Harrisonburg : Herald Press, 2018. | Includes bibliographical
   references.
Identifiers: LCCN 2018026337| ISBN 9781513802343 (pbk. : alk. paper) |
   ISBN 9781513802572 (hardcover : alk. paper)
Subjects: LCSH: Bible--Introductions. | Bible--Hermeneutics.
Classification: LCC BS475.3 .G66 2018 | DDC 220.6/1--dc23 LC record
   available at https://lccn.loc.gov/2018026337

THE BIBLE UNWRAPPED
© 2018 by Herald Press, Harrisonburg, Virginia 22803. 800-245-7894.
All rights reserved.
Library of Congress Control Number: 2018026337
International Standard Book Number: 978-1-5138-0234-3 (paperback);
978-1-5138-0257-2 (hardcover); 978-1-5138-0235-0 (ebook)
Printed in United States of America
Cover and interior design by Merrill Miller

22 21 20 19 18   10 9 8 7 6 5 4 3 2 1

To my parents, Steve and Pam,
who treasure Christ and nurture laughter,
and who had the gall to reply to complaints of boredom,
"Why don't you go read your Bible?"

CONTENTS

PART III: **Bringing It Home**

*Then Jesus did many other miraculous signs
in his disciples' presence,
signs that aren't recorded in this scroll.*

*But these things are written so that you will believe
that Jesus is the Christ, God's Son,
and that believing, you will have life in his name.*

JOHN 20:30-31

FOREWORD

The book you are about to read is a rare treasure. If you'll indulge me, I believe you will much better appreciate what I have to say about this remarkable book if I share a bit of my backstory.

I "got saved" on June 29, 1974, at a Pentecostal evangelistic service. I had just turned seventeen. It was a remarkably powerful experience, and I remember it like it was yesterday. For the previous four years I'd been living a "drugs, sex, and rock-and-roll" lifestyle, and doing so as a self-professed atheist. But I had recently been feeling increasingly empty on the inside. That night, throughout the twenty minutes or so that it took for a young woman from a local Bible school to deliver her sermon, I could feel my inner emptiness transforming into a profound yearning. I desperately needed the Jesus that she was talking about.

The moment the preacher finished an altar call, I hopped to my feet and marched to the altar. A man who was slightly older than me approached me and quietly explained what I needed to pray to "get saved." Then, after telling me to burn all my rock-and-roll albums—they were "devil music" and could cause me to lose my salvation—he gave me a new King James Bible and told me to make this book my "very best friend." "Devour it," he said. The Bible was 100 percent true, he informed me, and I should take it all literally.

Eager to feel as close to God as possible, I promised the man I would do so. Unlike my promise to destroy my collection of the devil's music, I followed through. Almost every morning and evening I spent thirty minutes to an hour reading my Bible. I even took it to school every day throughout my senior year in high school. I dutifully read it during lunch breaks, between classes, and even during classes when the teachers were boring me (which was more often than not).

All this sincere Bible reading didn't have the effect I'd been promised. Sure, I *occasionally* felt closer to God, but most of the time it either bored me, or confused me, or both.

Since I assumed that God intended us to start at the beginning, I dove into Genesis. And right out of the gate, I was puzzled. How come animals were created *before* humans in Genesis 1 but *after* humans in Genesis 2? And why did God need to give us two creation stories in the first place? Why does the Bible teach that everything was created in six days, when virtually all scientists agree that it took millions of years of evolution for humans to arrive on the scene?

Things only got worse when I moved on to Leviticus. Why on earth would God have his people sacrifice innocent animals and then go on and on, in excruciatingly gory detail, about how to do that? Who cares about all those endless nitpicky details surrounding the building of the tabernacle? And why would God insist that ancient Israelites not wear wool and cotton together, or sow different kinds of seeds in the same field, or eat shellfish or pork?

Other questions arose as I obediently continued trying to make the Bible "my best friend." Why did God make the Israelites his "chosen people"? Doesn't God love everybody? What's up with the Song of Solomon, which only served to intensify my struggle with lust? Why does Ecclesiastes sound like it was written by a depressed atheist? Why do so many psalms pray for God to exact terrible vengeance on enemies when Jesus teaches that we're to unconditionally love and forgive them? And why do we need four different versions of the life of Jesus? Shouldn't we expect a God-inspired book to get it right the first time?

The questions that disturbed me most, however, were generated from my discovery of just how grotesquely violent God's inspired book is. Why would God command his people to mercilessly annihilate entire populations of people? Why do so many heroes in the Bible kill so many people, often for really stupid reasons? Most disturbing of all, how could Jesus teach and model perfect love and total nonviolence in the Gospels—but then return someday, as Revelation seems to suggest, and angrily slaughter much of the world's population?

So just over a year after my euphoric conversion, I quit. By this time I was attending a university, and before completing my first semester I had completely lost my faith. When I finally concluded that I could no longer "believe the Bible," I assumed this meant I had to abandon all those other beliefs as well. The feelings of inner emptiness returned, with a vengeance. I struggled on and off with depression for the next nine months.

Since I'm writing this foreword, you've probably figured out that I found a way back into the faith. That's a story for another book. But I share all this to say: *How I wish I could have read this book forty-three years earlier!* (How inconsiderate of you, Meghan Good, to wait so long to be born!) I'm completely certain this book would have prevented my excruciating loss of faith.

It's not that *The Bible Unwrapped* addresses all the questions I had as a young man. Rather, it would have empowered me to find answers to my questions. Even more importantly, I would have discovered that I was often *asking the wrong questions*!

Reflecting an impressive depth and breadth of biblical and historical knowledge, and utilizing insightful analogies and compelling and often humorous stories, Good illuminates our understanding of Scripture by disclosing just what kind of book God inspired the Bible to be. (Hint: it's not at all what I was told as a new Christian, and not what most Christians are told.) She artistically and insightfully reviews the various kinds of literature we find in Scripture and fleshes out the value of each genre. With the insight of a scholar and the heart of a pastor, Good provides readers with the skills to discern how everything in Scripture contributes to the unfolding story of God's relationship with humanity. Most importantly, Good brilliantly unwraps the Bible to reveal that it is all about Jesus: the unsurpassable revelation of God.

Since finding my way back to the faith, I have read countless books that introduce readers to the Bible. I can honestly say that I have found none as enjoyable to read—without sacrificing anything by way of biblical scholarship—as this one. Nor do I recall ever finding a book on this topic that so clearly, and so thoroughly, covers so much ground in such a short amount of space. And I certainly have never come upon one that combines such a high degree of scholarship with an immensely practical orientation.

But there is one more thing I have to add to my praise of *The Bible Unwrapped*, and it is the thing that most surprised me, and most blessed me, about this masterpiece. I can't put my finger on what exactly brought about this unexpected blessing, but I suspect it has something to do with the artful and entertaining way Good writes—she is one of the best storytellers you will ever read or hear. And I'm certain it has something to do with the way the Spirit anoints her. Whatever the reason, I found that reading *The Bible Unwrapped* actually *intensified my own love of Scripture* precisely because it helped me better see the Savior whom I love through it.

No introduction to the Bible I've ever read has done that before. In fact, I've never dreamed of expecting this from any introduction to the Bible. I finished *The Bible Unwrapped* with a feeling of deep gratitude for the dedicated work of Meghan Good and for God for leading her and equipping her to do it so well.

When you finish *The Bible Unwrapped*, I have no doubt that your understanding of Scripture will be increased and that you will be much better equipped to apply it to your life and to our troubled world. I pray this book will both deepen your love of Scripture and your love for the One to whom all Scripture points.

—Gregory A. Boyd, senior pastor of Woodland Hills Church and author of numerous books

INTRODUCTION

Imagine a small cabin in a vast forest.

The cabin is simple and familiar. It's filled with television and premade dinners and a terrifying backlog of messages demanding an urgent response. It's composed, in other words, of all the usual clutter and clamor that make up modern life.

The forest outside the cabin is wild and wonderful and strange. It contains sunny glens and cool, quiet clefts, morning glories that bloom for just one perfect day and cedars that tower and count ages likes breaths. The forest stretches out in every direction for miles beyond counting.

The cabin: this is the world as we know it, the stuff of our ordinary, daily human realities. The forest is the infinite, eternal Life of God, the full Reality of all that truly exists.

It would be possible to live your whole life in the cabin never realizing what is outside its four solid walls. Except that one of those walls contains a glass window, and through that window you catch glimpses of a beckoning Beyond.

The glass window is the Bible.

The point of a window is not the pane of glass in and of itself. One purpose of a window is the light it sheds on everything inside. Another is the view it provides of that which lies beyond its frame. A good window draws the gaze through itself, unobstructed; it is a servant of the landscape outside. In similar fashion, the Bible is not an end in itself. It is not God. It is not the forest. It is the opening through which we catch glimpses of the strange and wonderful Really Real and begin to imagine what it could mean to step outside our walls and meet it face-to-face.

But this is the point at which many readers of the Bible get confused.

Some mistake the window for the view. Their gaze stops at the surface of the pane. Instead of recognizing the extraneous, external Reality of the forest, they start to believe the entire world is contained inside the glass. Instead of approaching the window as an opening to the living forest's dynamism, they approach it like a two-dimensional painting that is no more than it depicts. The window in this case becomes a graven image—an idol, not an invitation.

Others become cynical about the dust, chips, and warps that a window which has weathered thousands of years inevitably accumulates. They decide that a view touched by cracks or dust is of no use at all, and they turn their backs on the window to stare at an empty wall. They attempt to hypothesize about what lies without, from their experience of what lies within. Having forsaken the window, they end up gazing in a mirror, seeing only a reflection of themselves and the room in which they're standing.

Both of these approaches to the Bible reflect a fundamental misunderstanding of the Bible's role. The primary purpose of Scripture is to disclose precisely what lies beyond the pages of Scripture: Jesus Christ, the Word made flesh, the Risen One who lives to be encountered. The early Christians believed that the Bible was rightly read when it led to contemplation of, and participation in, nothing less than Jesus himself.[1]

This means we don't just read Scripture—we read through Scripture like a window. We read until the ink becomes transparent, a portal to a place where the living Christ is waiting to be met. As interpreters of the Bible, our job is to clean the glass, clearing the accumulated fog of historical distance and misperception, so that we and others with us have a clearer view outside.

This book is an exploration of what it looks like to read the Bible this way—as a window, as a portal. In part 1, we begin with a broad examination of the window and its frame. We will explore how this window was formed in the first place and do a broad topographical survey of what we see when we gaze through it. In part 2 we will acquire a few of the tools that are particularly useful in helping to clear the glass and sharpen our view. In part 3 we'll begin to suggest what it takes to move from being observers to being participants in the wider world of God. All three parts are interspersed with stories that illustrate how the Bible comes alive as we gaze through it.

The rustling, billowing Spirit of God sets and resets the scene before us, somehow both ancient and always new. But the Bible's purpose is not fulfilled until knowledge gives way to encounter. The true end of Scripture is eternal life, beginning here and now, as we are drawn outside the confines of our musty cabin world to play in the windblown wilds of God.

PART I

OPENING THE BOOK

1

THE GREAT "WHAT IF"
A Good Place to Start

All knowledge begins with a leap of faith. The love a parent has for a child involves something more than pure biological self-interest. When I roll out of bed tomorrow morning, the law of gravity will still be in effect. The neighbor's cats, however shifty looking, are not actively plotting humanity's extermination.

I cannot strictly prove any of these assertions. But the evidence in their favor seems compelling enough that I am willing to believe them and to get on with living as if they are true. And ongoing experience continually reinforces my sense of the accuracy of these conclusions. Even the most committed scientist bent over her laboratory microscope must choose, as a condition of her work, to take certain things for granted: that her senses can be trusted; that her measurements correspond with something true within the shape of reality; that the natural laws that applied yesterday will apply the same tomorrow.

Every person approaches the world with some fundamental assumptions about reality and how it operates.

Some believe that the material world is all there truly is, that everything which exists must be accessible (at least in theory) to scientific observation and impartial measurement. The universe is a closed system in which no outside forces intervene. Religious claims are no more than the remnant of primitive superstitions.

Others imagine that there might well be a cosmic Designer who exists but who is functionally irrelevant to human affairs. This divine being, whoever he or she might be, is either utterly indifferent to the world or firmly committed to a policy of noninterference. Either way, human beings and human beings alone determine the course and outcome of history. If God enters into the conversation at all, it is only as an inspirational ideal or existential guarantor of some universal intuition of justice.

Still others picture a God in heaven and humans on earth with a great chasm in between. Under normal circumstances, both parties remain cordoned off on their side of the cosmic divide. But on rare occasions, in response to prayers or when things simply grow desperate enough, God tears through the wall of time and space and nudges things around a bit in a rare, one-off occurrence often called "a miracle." In such a world, the primary goal of religious activity is to induce, or otherwise equip, God to break the barrier and intervene.

None of these descriptions of the world can be definitively proved or disproved—they can only be accepted as the best representation of the available evidence. Even skepticism itself is a form of belief; to doubt one picture of the world is to begin believing otherwise.[1] No one, religious or not, escapes the orbit of faith.

Since all of us, in one way or another, are already taking a leap on something, we have nothing to lose in conducting a simple thought experiment. Let's suppose, just to see where it leads us, that there is another way to put together the available evidence. Suppose the universe is animated, down to its bosons and quarks, by the very breath of God. Suppose that it's all this way—suppose that all of it *is*—simply because God sees it. Suppose superheated gas and stardust spun into the first cells of life beneath the hands of a masterful Artist. Suppose that Artist, who delights in new frontiers and changing forms, didn't want to go away and settle into distant observation but instead stayed on to relate, to communicate, to participate in an ongoing process of creative emergence.

This is the Bible's bold hypothesis, its grand leap of faith: that there never was any closed cosmic system from which God could be barred or into which God has to break as a stranger. From the very beginning until now, the Bible posits, the Maker's fingers have been dug into the soil of creation. God is closer to the world than any of us have dared imagine, speaking to it and hearing its voice, moving it and somehow being moved by it. No human being has ever seen or known a world absent of God; we can't even begin to imagine one.

According to the Bible, God has made a choice to bind God's self to humanity—to love, listen, guide, disrupt, create, relate, and leave us room to choose. History is neither fated by some preformed divine script nor given over to the tyranny of human whims. God acts, and we respond. God speaks, and we talk back. This communication, this interchange, is happening constantly, with ordinary people just like us. History is what takes shape on the wheel between our palms and God's as we both press the turning clay of time and space.

The world's story began with God's decisive action and will end with God's decisive action, the Bible suggests. But everything in between is relationship, a dialogue, a dynamic dance between God and humans as we respond to each other's movements. The dips and turns this story takes along the way vary greatly depending on the extent to which we attune ourselves to the divine music and on how well we learn to follow our divine Partner's lead.

There is no way to objectively "prove" this is the truth about the world. None of us has the luxury of standing at an impartial distance. We can only form our judgments as people situated in the middle of a story. The Bible mounts no elaborate philosophical arguments in defense of its great leap. Instead, it simply offers witnesses from the field—testimony from people who heard a Voice they weren't expecting that both broke them and remade them, people who watched with their own eyes as death suddenly turned, impossibly, into life. The testimony of a community who followed a cloud out of slavery and into freedom, a community whose experience could not be accounted for by the sum of its constituent human parts.

All knowledge begins with some leap of faith. Our journey with the Bible begins with willingness to entertain a simple "what if." What if God had something to say? What if human beings were capable of hearing? More than that, what if God was closer than our breathing? What if God wore feet and walked our streets, caked in the dust of our neighborhoods?

When we come to the Bible, we hear the stories of people much like us who dared to make the leap, to live as if all this were the truth about the world, and to see what resulted—people who found far more than they first set out looking for. If we sit with their stories long enough, engage with them curiously enough, we might find that our senses begin to pick up sights and sounds and scents we never perceived before.

We might even catch ourselves walking around and glancing over our shoulder, wondering what such a God-on-the-loose could be up to now.

2

QUANTUM LEAPS
Reasons for Reading

For some who grew up in the Bible Belt—who cut their teeth on the back of a church pew and who could make out like bandits in hymn-lyric Jeopardy—a chapter on why the Bible matters might seem unnecessary, and maybe even borderline heretical. But I'll let you in on a secret—you're not alone if you have doubts about the Bible's enduring cogency. A few weeks into teaching a class on interpreting the Bible, a woman who'd been a regular church attender for more than sixty years burst into my office. She threw her Bible on my desk, shouting, "I've been reading this, and it's outrageous! Do you even know what's in there?!" It turned out she'd just discovered the book of Joshua.

It's not uncommon for people to pull me aside and confess, with a spark of anger or tears in their eyes, that they gave up on the Bible years ago. Many of them are well-respected pastors and leaders in their local churches. The Bible's obscure laws and bloody tales seem irrelevant at best and offensive at worst. "Can't I just get on with loving God and doing good," they ask, "and let this outdated book go?" Perhaps the most common question teenagers ask me about religion is, "Why should I even care what the Bible has to say?"

If you are one of those who quietly (or maybe not so quietly) wonder if this ancient book deserves its hype, know that there are many people out there who share your questions. But despite the undeniable challenges involved, I'd suggest at least a couple of key reasons why the Bible is still worth deep consideration.

First, seeking God without the Bible is sort of like trying to discover the principles of quantum physics . . . from scratch. Since God is always at work in the world, it is certainly possible to learn real things about God through direct, personal experience, whether through prayer or reflection on situations you've encountered, or simply by gazing on the mountains. There's no doubt about it—God shows up.

But here's the thing: if you started traveling today, using the fastest vehicle current technology can build, it would take you 225,000,000,000,000 years to reach the edge of the universe. And that's just the universe we know about. If it stopped expanding. If your mind rebels at even the suggestion of such vastness, consider this: it's safe to assume that the truth about God, well, is even bigger. Even if we somehow manage to be exactly right in every conclusion we draw about God and the cosmos from our own experience—and religious history suggests that is an unlikely prospect—in one short lifetime we'll never personally manage to see more than a few grains of sand in the ocean of God. There are aspects of this vast universe of God that will always lie far beyond human access unless God chooses to reveal them, to bring them out of the reaches of space and directly into our view.

If everyone had to rediscover gravity for themselves starting with Newton's apple, our knowledge of the world would
be limited indeed. When we open the Bible, we stand on the
shoulders of giants who have come before us. As science has
Galileo, Curie, and Einstein, faith has Sarah, Ezekiel, and
John—people who didn't just possess acute spiritual sensitiv-
ities but were active recipients of God's own self-revelation.
Above all, we have the witness of Jesus, who was uniquely
positioned to reveal the mind of God. When we come to the
Bible, we have a chance to lay our own small grains of insight
along this larger shoreline. Instead of struggling one by one,
lifetime after lifetime, to draw together enough tiny scraps of
insight to ascertain some small truth that merits confidence,
we start out with the fundamental principles already known,
with a whole wealth of knowledge already in hand.

Second, it's crucial to remember that every individual, every community, every culture, and every generation has its
own biases and blind spots. Just as your own personal experience of God and the world opens you to particular insights, it
closes you to others. Even pooling our experiences and ideas
with a diverse group of friends is not enough to save us, because there are things in the water of history that all of us
are drinking that affect us collectively whether we perceive
their flavor or not. Those who set out in search of God independent of the Bible almost invariably end up finding a God
who looks very much like themselves—a God who shares
their tastes and politics, their assumptions and ambitions, the
trending philosophies of their time.

When we come to the Bible, we look at God through the
eyes of ages and cultures that don't share our own presump-
tions and preoccupations. When we interpret, we enter into

conversation not just with the biblical writers but with thousands of years of readers who have their own experiences, concerns, and perspectives. In doing this—in humbling ourselves to engage this conversation—we are checked in our temptation to bow to a god who is no more than the spirit of our age, a god made in the image of our own particular distortions. We glimpse truths that our companions-in-time, who are blinded by the same modern lights and myths that we are, are simply not in a position to tell us.

Finally, and hardest to pin down, is the naked power of the book itself. Literature attains status as "classic" when it speaks in such a way that generation after generation reading it gains insight into the world or the human condition. The Bible is somewhat like classic literature in this, yet also qualitatively more. Millennia of readers testify that those who listen carefully find themselves addressed by a voice beyond the page that somehow penetrates and breaks things open. God, in some strange and unique way, actually talks here. And where God starts talking, chains are broken, wounds are healed, and whole worlds are upended.

If you haven't experienced this phenomenon for yourself, hearing other people talk about their experience with the Bible can feel a lot like looking at an autostereogram. More commonly known as a "Magic Eye" image, an autostereogram is a two-dimensional image containing a buried 3-D scene that emerges when the page is viewed with two eyes properly aligned. It's as if everyone around you is saying "Look, there's a dolphin! Right there in front of you!" when all you can see is a blur of random colors.

You could, of course, doubt your witnesses, insist there's nothing here to see except what's inside people's own heads.

But consider—when person after person standing on the same plot of land feels the ground shift beneath them, it's reasonable to ask if there's a fault line lying under the surface. If enough people over enough time sit before the same book and feel the earth surge under them, it's at least worth asking whether there might be a powerful force moving beneath the pages.

If you haven't yet seen the Bible "pop"—if you haven't glimpsed the dolphin—it's at least worth considering that what you might need is not new friends but a new approach to looking.

On this count, all I can really do is add my own voice to the two-thousand-year-long chain of other witnesses. I have read many books in my life, some of them dozens of times apiece. But only one book has time and time again caused the earth to shift beneath me. Only one has made me laugh and cry and shout and fall in love. Only one has turned enemies into friends and fear into courage and despair into hope.

3

BEYOND BASIC INSTRUCTIONS
What Kind of Book

In a church I visited regularly as I was growing up, a large banner hung on the wall by the stage. It boldly proclaimed, "BIBLE: Basic Instructions Before Leaving Earth." I stared at that banner for years and never thought to question its message. Its pithy statement captured exactly what I imagined the Bible to be—sort of like a Roomba owner's manual, only for the human soul. Applying the Bible was a matter of cracking the manufacturer's code so you knew which buttons to press, in exactly what sequence, to make this thing called life run right (and not choke and die on a rug).

The trouble was, like many Bible readers before me, I discovered over time that such a characterization of the Bible's nature was strangely mismatched with its contents. To begin with, it's hard to imagine any definition of "basic" that includes detailed directions for constructing gold lampstands or for determining the cud-chewing habits of your future steak. Yet both these subjects occupy significant sacred real estate. Meanwhile, topics that seem of rather fundamental relevance to faithful living—say, how to figure out what kind of work you were meant for, or how to raise a God-loving kid who doesn't hate your guts—aren't covered in any direct way at all.

This isn't to suggest that the Bible contains no practical directives relevant to everyday living. The Bible offers many helpful insights on such important subjects as managing money, maintaining relationships, and keeping your tongue from wrecking your life (counsel surely as relevant in the age of Twitter as it ever was). But still, if the primary purpose of the Bible were to efficiently convey the most basic, universally relevant knowledge necessary to maintain a well-ordered life, most of us would expect a very different kind of book. We'd want a little more quick reference index, a little less poetry; a little more guidance on romance and dating, a little less detail on how to build a giant ark without power tools.

One of the strangest things about the Bible is that, instead of sticking to grand universals, the Bible is often shockingly particular. It regularly addresses *this* particular person in *this* specific situation, which might never again be precisely replicated. Exodus 23:4 explains what to do if your enemy loses his donkey—a situation that a resident of, say, Chicago, has only slightly better odds of experiencing than being gored to death by an ox (a scenario that Exodus 21 helpfully addresses). Both 1 Corinthians and Romans spill a great deal of ink exploring the ethics of eating meat that has been sacrificed to idols—a major dilemma for people navigating first-century Roman culture but not one likely to come up today in your average Brooklyn deli. The author of 1 Timothy instructs the recipient of his letter, "Don't drink water anymore, but use a little wine because of your stomach problems and your frequent illnesses" (1 Timothy 5:23)—a prescription whose universal applicability seems ambiguous at best.

Some of the Bible's clearest commands are patently impossible to obey. "Say hello to the brothers and sisters in Laodicea," Colossians 4:15 instructs—a command difficult to comply with, as the referenced city was destroyed during the Middle Ages. The silent consensus of Christian history simply seems to give us permission to sidestep other commands—for example, the Deuteronomy 21:18-21 command to stone rebellious sons or the command given in 1 Peter 5:14 for Christians to "greet each other with the kiss of love." While it might seem intuitively obvious that some commands in the Bible do not apply to us, in practice it's actually quite difficult to articulate how we know which ones do and which ones don't.

Then there are the difficulties with the term *instructions*. The Bible is broadly divided into two sections, commonly called the Old and New Testaments. Around 40 percent of the Old Testament and an even higher percentage of the New is made up of narrative. And nearly a third of the Bible is composed of poetry—including an entire book dedicated to lauding the goodness of sex (Song of Songs—yep, put this book down and go look it up). Yet very little biblical narrative or poetry is "instructional" in a clear and straightforward fashion.

Take the Judges 11 tale of a man who makes a wartime vow that he keeps by killing his own daughter. It is far from obvious what the directive of such a story might be. Are these parenting instructions? Is this advice on keeping your word? Or when to be smart enough to break it? Or consider the infamous conquest stories, in which God's people slaughter the populations of entire cities on their way to claiming divinely promised property. The movement from narrative to instruction here seems hazard prone at best. And following the example of Song of Songs by informing your beloved that her hair is "like a flock of goats" and her teeth are "like newly shorn ewes" is unlikely to achieve your desired result.

Biblical passages like these might well serve a vital purpose, and we'll explore some of the possibilities as we go forward in this book. But the pedagogical value they possess is quite distant from the clear directive of step-by-step instructions or from the prescriptive clarity of a universal law. The "point" in many cases is far from obvious. In fact, while some biblical texts offer answers, others simply seem to complicate the questions.[1]

But if the shape of the Bible does not neatly conform to the paradigm of *Human Life for Dummies*, what does its unique combination of ancient laws, harrowing tales, private letters, and epic poetry actually add up to? What kind of book is this really? The reality is a bit more complex than that suggested by the five-word banner from my childhood. Perhaps the best place to begin exploring the Bible's nature is with what seems most obvious: whatever else we may have in the Bible, at the broadest level what we find there is a story. The Bible tells the story of a series of encounters between God and humanity.

From the dawn of human existence, long before the Bible's first pages were penned, God has been reaching toward human beings, and human beings back toward God. Humans have struggled to comprehend God's character and being, God's good desires for them, and God's dreams for the whole created order. God has struggled to get humans to listen to the revelation of these things. Whatever else it does, the Bible witnesses to this bidirectional pursuit.

Not every story in the Bible reflects what ought to be. Not everything that happens in the pages of the Bible does so because it should. Not every word spoken by someone in the Bible comes stamped with divine endorsement. This is no fairy-tale or snow-globe world. The Bible tells the story of what *is*. It's the true story of a world where hearing is imperfect, where motives are mixed, where evil exists, where bias lingers, where good intentions can go wildly astray. And where God persists in showing up.

There is little question that the pursuit to which the Bible witnesses has met with mixed results. Sometimes the divine hand reaches down in a unilateral act of rescue. Sometimes it's ignored or brushed away, with catastrophic results. Sometimes two reaching hands—God's and a human's—meet each other, and miracles are born. The Bible tells all of these kinds of stories. We hear what people speak to God. We learn what they hear back. We watch them try and fail and learn and start all over again. We see them searching and being found—sometimes even despite themselves.

The Bible's story isn't neat, because this kind of pursuit never is. It's messy and confusing and frequently uncomfortable. But it's precisely the blood and sweat and tears and questions that certify the Bible's trustworthiness. This is the story of real life—raw and complicated and sacred. By immersing ourselves in Scripture's messy stories, and by daring to call them God-breathed and holy, we are reminded that if God can be here, God can be anywhere. Even with broken people like us. Even in our cracked and jagged world. Even in our own up-and-down, back-and-forth, missing-and-reaching stories.

4

THE WORLD IN COLOR
Shaping Biblical Imagination

If the Bible is a story, it is also something more: it's a book that dares to make an authoritative claim on life. Between the poems and proverbs and parables, a portrait takes shape of who God is and what exactly God desires. The Bible suggests that to learn to walk with God and love the things that God loves is to begin to live in sync with the world's true design.

This description of the Bible—an introduction to God and to the shape of the "with God" life—is something rather different from "basic instructions." From time to time I fantasize about possessing a handbook that would answer every problem with a clear three-step process. Secure a great husband, according to the book of Ruth: (1) don your best dress; (2) sneak up to a man's bed after he's spent a long evening partying with friends; (3) uncover his feet and lie down and wait to see what he says. (Check out Ruth 3 to catch that story.)

Of course, the trouble with instruction manuals is how quickly they go out of date. A 2018 atlas could offer you a detailed guide for driving from New York to Los Angeles. The instructions might be absolutely perfect on the day they were laid out. But what happens when traffic patterns change? Or a tree falls in the way? Or when cars are replaced by hovercrafts? The precise sequence of turns that once would have carried you safely to your destination could now lead you far astray, even send you skidding into wreckage. The goal, the ultimate destination, remains exactly the same. But the ability to get there safely requires a certain ingenuity—the ability to navigate previously unknown obstacles and adapt to new terrain.

The Bible's opening sequence in Genesis 1, which describes God's creation of the world, could leave some readers with the impression that everything is finished, tied off, completed—like a highway laid down once, never to be altered again: "God said, 'Let there be light.' And so light appeared" (verse 3). If this is the case, turn-by-turn directions would seem the perfect communication tool. But Genesis 2 immediately complicates this picture of creation by depicting God playing in the mud of the newly minted earth. Humans are on the scene now, but God remains in the world as well, and the creative work is still unfolding.

The scene in Genesis 2 always reminds me a bit of kids tinkering in a sandbox. God forms a creature and hands it to Adam and asks, "What do you think we should call it?" Adam replies, "It's a spiny lumpsucker!" And that becomes its name. Presumably this is about the moment God decides it might be time to bring Eve around, if only for a second opinion.

In Genesis 2, human beings are not merely passive observers of God's work in the world; they are active participants in the creative vocation of God. They—and we—are assigned the task of cultivating soil that is pregnant with divine possibilities ("The Lord God took the human and settled him in the garden of Eden to farm it and take care of it"). This vocation, given humanity in Genesis 2:15, is not mechanical assembly line work—that of stamping identical cogs pumping out of a machine. It's creative, nurturing work. It's the vocation of a gardener who tends living, growing things—a vocation not just of preservation but of emergence.

The number and complexity of tasks and the variability of conditions demand that a gardener have a far more intimate knowledge of her soil than a finite list of instructions would ever contain. The gardener must understand her soil's potential and vulnerabilities enough to recognize potential new threats, adapt to changing conditions, and cultivate flourishing in all seasons. What she needs is a mind that is attuned to the nature of the earth itself.

This is why, I believe, the Bible takes a much more ambitious approach to human formation than a simple rule book could provide. God is shaping not automated drones but artists in the image of a Master. Now, an artist must begin by learning the essential rules of her craft. A sculptor won't get far if she denies the nature of clay, refusing to keep it moist, firing it in ways that make it crack. Similarly, there are basic rules for how God's world operates—principles of moral gravity, if you will, whose defiance is quite costly. Infidelity, to word or relationship, breaks things. Webs of deception trap the weaver. The Bible points out some of these essential principles so that we can work with the nature of our clay rather than against it.

But rules alone are not enough! An artist needs imagination, a vision of what can be. The Bible is more than only a story—it's a story moving us and the world somewhere. It's a revelation of who God is, of what God loves, of how the world is shaped. It's an invitation to a relationship, an apprenticeship in God's creative, nurturing vocation. The Bible provides the essential information we need to creatively lean in. We were made for so much more than paint-by-number religion. We were made to cast the dreams of God on many different canvases, in all the diverse shapes and vibrant, Spirit-saturated colors of true life. The Bible trains our eye for the divine aesthetic and then sends us out with a brush in hand to paint with the help of the Master.

Between the lines of its obscure laws and strange and unexpected stories, the Bible forms inspired imagination for the God-shaped possibilities of the world. In it we learn what God's activity has looked like in the past so that we will recognize it when it is unfolding right in front of us. We discover what God sounds like so that we can hear when God continues to speak. We learn what God loves so we can be alert for opportunities to stir that delight. We learn what God dreams of so we can begin to live that dream. The Bible shapes imagination for how God can be encountered in ordinary life and for how we can cooperate with God in encouraging the flourishing of all creation.

It turns out that the strange particularity of the Bible's address that we noted earlier—God's word to this person, in this place, at this time, in this specific situation—is powerful precisely because it is the particular that shapes imagination for the universal. The same God who talked to ancient farmers about paying their day laborers before sunset so their families would have dinner that night (Deuteronomy 24:14-15) has something to say as well to modern office managers about how they care for the needs of the temp. God is at work not just everywhere but *somewhere in particular*. God tends not just every bloom but *this one*, in its unique soil and shape and condition. We are being formed by the Bible to join God not just in general but in the specificity of genuine care, in all the hereness and nowness of the particular bit of creation with which we have been uniquely entrusted.

In Romans 12:2, an early Christian leader named Paul writes, "Don't be conformed to the patterns of this world, but be transformed by the renewing of your minds so that you can figure out what God's will is—what is good and pleasing and mature." The patterns of this world run across our news feed every minute of the day—cycles of fear, greed, isolation, and violence that all the intellect of all the nations can't seem to find a way beyond. But those who are shaped by the Bible are formed for a more beautiful imagination. We imagine a community where no one is poor, because what belongs to one is a gift for all. We imagine conflict where enemies defend each other's interests. We imagine marriage—and sex—characterized by mutual submission, where each partner guards the other's joy as if it were their own. We imagine a justice defined not by matching wounds but by the healing of what's broken. We dare to imagine a genuine friendship, a true companionship with God.

Through Scripture our imaginations are shaped, page by page, into the imagination of Christ. We learn to see past the surface of the broken soil around us to the small but potent seeds of divine possibility, which have been planted within and are waiting to be cultivated. This vision of faithful living is so much bigger than a rote performance of a finite set of religious rules. The Bible's invitation is to a life of creative, risk-taking engagement. Its movement drives us toward a relationship still unfolding and a story still being written—in us, in our children's children, and in generations yet to come.

STORYTIME

Unwrapping Joshua 5:13–6:27

JOSHUA IS A young man whose star is clearly on the rise.

Joshua's mentor, Moses, is a living legend, the greatest leader in his people's history. Moses challenged the pharaoh of Egypt to a duel—and won! He rescued hundreds of thousands of people from slavery. He parted a body of water just by holding out his walking stick. He delivered the Ten Commandments after speaking face-to-face with God. And Joshua has been handpicked as his successor.

When the time finally comes for Moses to pass the baton, he commissions Joshua in front of everyone: "I got them out of Egypt; now you'll get them into the Promised Land." Then Moses dies, and the community offers him this modest eulogy: "No one has ever shown the mighty power or performed the awesome deeds that Moses did in the sight of all Israel." All right then, Joshua— you're up! It's like being asked to solo right after Pavarotti.

Joshua's first task is to claim the city of Jericho, the gateway to the land he plans to conquer for his people. This is no small challenge, as Jericho, like most ancient cities of any importance, is surrounded by enormous walls that are meant to shield it from exactly the kind of invasion that Joshua is planning.

On the eve of Joshua's leadership debut, a messenger of God shows up for a talk. The messenger says to him, "Take off your sandals, for the place where you are standing is holy." As it happens, in the original Hebrew, these are almost exactly the same words God had spoken to Moses from a burning bush on the first day of his career—right before Moses led the slaves out of Egypt with ten plagues and some crazy waterworks. You can almost see the fireworks go off in Joshua's head as he connects the dots— "Wait a minute, that's exactly what you said to . . . Yes! Hot dog! Now it really begins! I wonder who will play me when the movie comes out . . ."

Joshua is excited, ready for his mission: "So now what, God? What will it be? Moses's first assignment was to turn a staff into a snake. Then he got to send plagues of frogs and lice and be led by a pillar of fire. What do you have in mind for me? Turning a hat into a tarantula? Hordes of angry scorpions that attack on my command? Lightning bolts falling at my word? Please tell me there will be lightning bolts."

God's messenger replies, "Okay, here's your assignment, Joshua. What God wants you to do is . . . walk in circles around the city of Jericho thirteen times."

Say what?

"Seriously? You've got to be kidding me, God! Give me something else to do. Anything! I'll dig tunnels under the city. I'll make a battering ram to beat down the gates. I'll even start chipping away at those walls with a spoon. At least then I'll have something to show at the end of the day for my labor. Anything but walking in circles!"

But God says circles, so circles it is.

The first time Joshua's people, the Israelites, appear on the horizon, marching toward the city of Jericho, the residents are terrified. A huge foreign army is standing on their doorstep! The Israelites march up to the city gate and stomp around the walls, blasting away on their trumpets of war (because the harps they tried first, well, just didn't quite set a conquering mood). The people of Jericho huddle in their houses, shaking in their sandals.

But then the trumpets stop blowing, and the Israelites walk away. At first the people of Jericho think, "Those Israelites are just messing with our minds. They'll be back tomorrow to finish the job." And the Israelites do come back the next day. They march around the walls, blasting their trumpets. The people all tremble some more. But again, nothing happens. It's the same on the third day. And the fourth. By the fifth day, you can imagine the people of Jericho are standing on top of their thick city walls, tossing rotten figs and shouting, "Sixth time's the charm! You know who said that? Nobody, like, ever. Hey smart guys, in case you haven't noticed, walking in circles ain't exactly a game-changing strategy."

You'd better believe the Israelites are thinking the same thing. Joshua is probably sitting alone in his tent with his hands over his face, feeling like a total idiot. Everyone knows the definition of insanity is doing the same thing over and over and expecting a different result. If the wall didn't fall the first time they went around it, why on earth would the thirteenth time be any different? No one ever got anywhere by walking in circles.

* * * * *

There's something about this story that feels painfully familiar to many seekers-after-God. Maybe once upon a time you set out on a spiritual journey with a great sense of resoluteness, expecting that big things would result—mountains would move or walls would crumble and all that jazz. You prayed. You started reading your Bible and made it at least halfway through Leviticus. You might have even gone to church. You rescued cats from trees and carried people's groceries.

But after a while you started to worry about the lack of discernable results. There seemed to be little proof of return on all that effort and investment. Perhaps you started to feel that you were mostly just going in circles, treading the same old ground again and again without getting anywhere. Maybe you were tempted to give up. Maybe you actually did.

Here's the thing: God does not seem to share our preoccupation with efficiency. A life of faith is much like a great road trip—the point isn't just where you're going but whom you're going with and the relationships that form on the journey. Sometimes the long way around is the most direct path to the true end.

Spiritual practices like prayer or worship or reading the Bible are exercises in walking circles, round and round, wearing deep grooves in the sidewalk. They often seem at first—even for a long time—to be achieving nothing at all.

But there's something worth noting . . .

Earthquakes (some of them, at least) happen when two tectonic plates that have been pushing against each other for ages without moving finally build up enough pressure that rock abruptly breaks. Entire cities crumble with the force of the sudden movement. Life with God is a lot like that. You don't have to know where you are going. You don't have to see where the pathway leads. You don't have to be certain of what difference it makes. Sometimes all that is required is to just keep walking, keep reading, keep talking, just keep pressing against the rock.

Twelve times you may walk around that circle with God and feel that you've gotten absolutely nowhere. But remember Joshua's story, and take heart: sometimes, on the thirteenth time around, walls really do fall down.

5

BECOMING BATMAN
Biblical Origins

I've always been a sucker for a good origin story—how Batman became Batman, who decided "blue raspberry" was a flavor, what sequence of tragically misguided thoughts led to the invention of the crinoline. Many people, if they've thought about it at all, suppose the Bible's origin story must involve something along the lines of a few religiously super-powered men equipped with James Bond–style earpieces sitting alone in a darkened room and receiving divine dictation.

But in fact, between the two covers of the Bible we have sixty-six books, each with its own origin story of who put it to paper and when and how. The Ten Commandments are boldly described in the book of Exodus as carved into stone by the finger of God. However, this wasn't exactly the standard mode of receiving divine mail. For other parts of the Bible, God's communication travels along paths of transmission that appear a bit more winding.

The Bible's oldest stories were first transmitted orally. They were family stories, the sort passed around the holiday table, one generation to the next, about how great-great-grandfather Methuselah (you know, the one with the weird big toe) had once seen God act. Of course, most of us as moderns have played enough games of "telephone" to develop reasonable concerns about the reliability of messages passed by word of mouth. But preliterate cultures had a knack for memorization that those of us who take for granted perennial access to all the knowledge in the universe as recalled by Google can hardly even conceive. Stories were told with rhythms and repetitions and other memory patterns built in, enabling them to be transmitted over time with an incredible level of accuracy.[1] As centuries passed and literacy increased, editors eventually wove these ancient memories into written collections, some of which are included in the Old Testament.

These stories are therefore not the product of the hand of a single author but of generations of people who recounted again and again particular tales about God's activity that continued to influence their real lives. The stories they retold were the ones that made a difference, the ones so big, so defining, and sometimes so dramatic that they could not be forgotten. Each new generation saw the significance and application of the stories slightly differently, and in some cases their distinct insights helped shape how the story was told. In this entire process in which stories were told and retold under the stars and around campfires, God was present, speaking.

Some books of the Bible explicitly state that they are drawing on material derived from other written sources. Kings and Chronicles, for example, assess the monarchal periods of the nations of Judah and Israel using historical records derived from "the annals of the kings" (see one such reference in 1 Kings 14:19 NIV). In the prologue to his gospel, Luke describes the extensive research process he undertook to ensure that the stories of Jesus he records are reliable and authentic—a process that included looking at other written compilations (see Luke 1:1-4). In this process of careful research and reflective study, God was present, speaking.

The book of Psalms contains prayers composed by individuals at the end of their rope, as well as songs that communities sang on their way to worship or at the ascension of a new king. Some of the biblical proverbs are quite similar to sayings circulating in other ancient Near Eastern countries like Egypt. In this process—by which certain songs captured the hearts of generations and certain wisdom sayings emerged from the rest bearing a spark of divinely generated insight about the world's true shape—God was present, speaking.

The biblical prophets assert themselves boldly as messengers endued with divine authority—"Thus says the Lord," they often declare. But most prophets functioned in their own time primarily as preachers rather than writers. Many of their "books" come to us through the pens of generations of their students. The prophets' messages, delivered in previous historical contexts, interacted with the new historical situations of these students to produce an explosion of fresh prophetic insights. All of this is woven together in the final biblical tapestry. A conversation between generations of the faith community is unfolding inside the text itself. In this process of addressing and readdressing divine messages in a direct and timely way for each generation of hearers, God was present, speaking.

The stories and teachings of Jesus recorded in the Gospels first traveled orally through the eyewitness testimony of those whom Jesus taught or healed. The New Testament epistles (letters) started out as personal mail, passed along hand to hand through a network of friends. Christian leaders wrote to communities with whom they had some connection, addressing rumors, correcting problems, sharing news, and commending action. Those communities, who were helped by these letters, shared them with other communities who were facing similar struggles. In this process of sharing stories and mail, of working out how the teachings of Jesus applied to different cultures and situations, God was present, speaking.

The final book of the Bible, Revelation, describes a mystical sort of visionary experience. The imagery of the vision draws on seer John's intimate background knowledge of older books of the Bible like Daniel and Ezekiel to communicate deep truths about the cosmic stakes behind the scene of history. In this complex interplay of supernatural experience and biblically formed imagination, God was present, speaking.

Perhaps like me you've encountered a podcaster who punctuates every thought with the same catchphrase, like "Am I right?" Or perhaps you know a preacher whose sermon metaphors run too often to football and children for you to believe he's a bachelor whose main hobby is calligraphy. The biblical writers, just like the rest of us, have real personalities, life experiences, and voices and preferences and concerns that inevitably influence their work. Amos, a shepherd, uses metaphors of rescuing sheep from lions (Amos 3:12) and of locust consuming grass (Amos 7:1-2)—images as close to his daily life as hunting tacos or navigating traffic is to mine. Mark uses the word *immediately* with the kind of frequency that makes you suspect he's the sort of guy who owns several fidget spinners. Paul favors athletic and military metaphors and isn't opposed to a scathing verbal cut-down when occasion seems to warrant. The individual, fully human person-hood of the writers has shaped in visible ways the message we possess.

But Christians also make a more radical claim about this book. Christians claim that the voices of the individual authors are not the only voices heard here. The words may come through human minds and lips, but there is divine breath behind them. In this collection of songs, laws, proverbs, and stories, God is at work with wisdom and intent that goes beyond the human authors alone. The name given to God's involvement in this process is "inspiration."

Overall, the Bible makes surprisingly few direct claims about its own nature and composition. It claims that its words are more than ancient inkblots on a page and are actually alive and up to things—exposing secrets, cutting to the heart of matters, judging thoughts and intentions (Hebrews 4:12-13). It claims to be useful for teaching, showing mistakes, and equipping people to do good (2 Timothy 3:16-17). It claims that the prophets specifically were led by the Spirit of God in what they understood (2 Peter 1:20-21). But perhaps the most notable claim the Bible makes about itself is that Scripture is divinely inspired—a phrase which literally means "God-breathed" (see 2 Timothy 3:16).

Strangely enough, this term, *God-breathed*, is not a word for which we have any record prior to its appearance in the letter of 2 Timothy. Some scholars suggest this might be because the author of the letter invented the term to establish a deliberate contrast with the beliefs of other religions of his day.[2] Other religious groups in the Roman world believed that a spirit could possess the body of a worshiper, over-riding the person's mind and speaking directly through the worshiper's lips. This phenomenon was often called "ecstatic speech." But unlike the gods of these pagan religious cults, the God of Christians did not short-circuit the human brain, take over the mouth, or override the human personality. Rather, the human writers of the Bible brought their whole selves to the work—their personalities, their experiences, their concerns—and God brought God's self—God's insights, God's clarity, God's life. Where these two elements come together, incredible things result. Frail, clumsy human words, imperfect vessels that they are, fill up with the powerful, living address of God.

The story of how each book in the Bible moved from thought to word to page is as unique as the message within it. But however a book came to be, whether it was touched by few hands or many, whether it was written overnight or told and retold and edited over centuries, inspiration is the claim that God was involved in each step of the process, ensuring that what came out was more than the sum of the human parts. People speak in the Bible, and their unique voices and perspectives can be heard. But so can the distinctive voice of a communicating God.

6

THE BREATH TEST
The Process of Canonization

Of course, it's one thing to suggest that the God of the universe might theoretically have something to say, whether thousands of years ago or today. It's another thing to figure out exactly where God has really spoken. We've all probably met people who claimed to be hearing from God but who we suspected might simply be channeling the thoughts of their favorite news pundit. It's enough to make you wish there were some sort of divine breathalyzer test to definitively measure the amount of Spirit a person (or book) has partaken of.

This was, in essence, the challenge that faced the very first Christians. They knew that something amazing and completely unprecedented had occurred in Jesus. Word of Jesus' life, death, and resurrection began to spread as witnesses took their story to the streets. Documents describing these world-changing events started to circulate. But the early Jesus followers quickly recognized that not all storytellers or story interpreters were equally trustworthy. One group called the Gnostics claimed that Jesus had brought special revelation that was available only to a few initiated elites; you had to drink the Kool-Aid, so to speak, to be let in on the secrets. Other people, called Docetists, suggested that Jesus was not truly human, that his body was only an illusion. The more time passed and the further the Christian community got from the defining Jesus events, the more urgent it became to identify which voices could be trusted to recount those all-important events reliably.

It's popular today to imagine that the process of choosing which books ended up in the Bible involved some kind of Hollywood-worthy conspiracy. Some picture a small group of men in a room late at night, whispering plots to stamp out truths they found bothersome and feeding the fire, page by page, with all the books they didn't like. But the truth is, the early Christians involved in the process of canonization didn't see themselves as "choosing" an authoritative set of books. Rather, they simply saw themselves as recognizing which books were already functioning authoritatively in actual communities of real Christians.

The Christian church had inherited the Old Testament from their Jewish predecessors. The details of the Old Testament's compilation stretch back too far in history to be fully known with certainty, but it appears that the first books officially accepted as an authoritative collection were the first five books of the Bible—a set of books Jews called the Torah, or the Law. The next collection of books gathered seem to have been the Prophets, followed finally by a diverse class of books known as the Writings. Scripture, as Jesus and his followers knew it in the first century, probably contained all the books currently included in the Protestant Old Testament as well as an additional collection of books called the Apocrypha.

You might wonder where exactly this extra set of books went. Their status was the subject of intense debate at various points in history. The books of the Apocrypha were written slightly later than the rest of the Old Testament, after the period of the biblical prophets, and were generally judged to be valuable for Christians to read but less authoritative than the other scriptural books. The early church debated whether such a set of "second tier" books should be included in the formal Christian collection that was taking shape. The arguments in favor of their inclusion in the Bible, as an edifying but less authoritative collection than the rest, ultimately won out until the Protestant Reformation in the 1500s, when the Protestant reformers decided to remove these books. The Roman Catholic Church chose at that time to keep the Apocrypha in their Bible—while still maintaining the Apocrypha's secondary status. This is why, depending on what Bible you happen to be reading, you may or may not find this set of books within it.

The story of the New Testament's formation is better documented than that of the Old. The apostle Paul, who wrote much of the New Testament, was aware even in his own lifetime that many of his letters were being circulated beyond the communities to which he had addressed them (see Colossians 4:16). The apostles, who had followed Jesus and seen him after his resurrection, were judged by the early Christians to have at least as strong a case for authority as the Old Testament prophets did—after all, they'd been in position to hear firsthand from God-in-flesh! Their teachings were therefore given significant weight.

By the second century, a collection of Paul's letters was widely in use, and by the late second century, the four gospels we now have in our Bibles were circulating together as a set. The first attempt to establish a formal list of which books functioned as Christian authority came in 200 CE and was called the Muratorian Canon. It included all our current New Testament books except Hebrews, 1 & 2 Peter, and 3 John.

In considering which books should be included in the Christian canon, the early church weighed several key factors. They looked for books whose authors were reliable—in particular, people who knew Jesus firsthand or who had learned under someone who knew him. In keeping with their conviction that they weren't "establishing" authority but simply recognizing it, they looked for books that were widely accepted by Christians across the world, books that diverse churches were already reading and finding genuinely helpful. In terms of content, they looked for books aligned with what was known as "the rule of faith"—the fundamentals of the good news about Jesus that Christians had believed and preached as the heart of their message since the very first days after his resurrection.

The entire process of forming an authoritative collection of books took centuries. When the Christian canon was finally established in 397 CE, it was the result of generations of diverse communities testing documents for evidence that they witnessed to the truth about Jesus and that God was working in them to change hearts and lives.[1]

This process of canonization suggests one big, significant question: Why on one random day in 397 CE (or on whatever unknown date the Bible's last sentence was written) did God abruptly stop talking the way God had before? Did people just collectively and suddenly lose access to some divine radio signal that no one since that day has managed to pick up?

The truth is, God didn't stop talking. The signal is still going strong. History since 397 CE is full of stories of saints and martyrs, teenage girls and elderly farmers, who heard the voice of God addressing them and responded with acts of radical courage, faithfulness, and sacrifice. The closing of the biblical canon did not represent an end to God's capacity to speak to people, nor did it represent the end of people's capacity to listen. What the closing of the canon did was safeguard the essentials of the Christian story.

The foundation of the Christian faith is not a set of abstract philosophical or ethical ideas but a set of real historical events, God's definitive action in the world in Jesus Christ. This part of the story doesn't change and cannot be somehow "improved upon," because no one will ever be in a better position to describe these defining events, what happened and what it meant, than Peter, James, John, and friends—the people who were actually present as witnesses and interacted with Jesus himself. The closing of the canon preserved the integrity of their testimony, the integrity of the part of the story that sets the stage for all that follows.

But the first Christians also fully expected that God would continue to talk. The early church did not restrict the notion of "inspiration" to the Bible alone but applied the term to Christian leaders, to the decisions of councils, and even to tomb inscriptions.[2] The purpose of establishing a written canon was not to claim that the Bible was the only place God would ever communicate again, would ever fill words with Spirit-breath. The world never stops needing God's insights, and a living God never stops breathing. What the church needed was a way to measure how what people in the future believed God was saying lined up with who God had definitively revealed God's self in Jesus to be. That's what the Bible gave them.

The canon wasn't meant to eliminate all other voices; rather, it marked where God had been clearly heard and experienced in the past. By doing this, it provided a measuring stick by which to evaluate all other claims going forward. This is what a canon is—a ruler, a yardstick. While situations might change, God's essential character will not, nor will what God had done for the world in Jesus.

In forming the canon, the church certified, "We hear God here"—precisely so we would be able to hear God reliably everywhere God speaks. The church certified, "We saw God act then and there," so that we will know with confidence when we see God acting here and now.

7

WHEN PETS RAIN
Selecting a Translation

The experience of shopping for a Bible, whether online or in the aisle of your local bookstore, bears a distinct resemblance to perusing the topping bar at a froyo joint. The display of colors and textures can be both dazzling and overwhelming. Some call themselves "New" and others "Revised" or even "Amplified." They come in camouflage and Barbie pink. Some boldly claim to be for cowboys and others for soon-to-be brides. Perhaps like me you've stood there puzzling over the nuanced distinction between chocolate balls, chocolate drops, and chocolate chips, vaguely terrified you'll make a mistake and end up with a chocolate cricket. I mean, what could the difference between all these Bibles actually be, and which one will just tell you the straight-up truth about what God really said?

Here's the first thing to understand about the abundance of Bibles out there: God is committed to speaking the language of those whom God addresses. To a Mandarin speaker, God speaks Mandarin. To the Sentinelese, God speaks Sentinelese. To a twenty-first-century speaker of English, God speaks twenty-first-century English and not the language of

Beowulf that stymied many of us in high school. If a new language someday forms based entirely on emojis, then God will speak that too. The people of Israel, whose story the Bible tells, originally spoke Hebrew, and therefore Hebrew is the language in which most of the Old Testament is composed. Parts of two of the later Old Testament books—Daniel and Ezra—are written in Aramaic, the everyday language of Jesus himself. The New Testament is written in Greek, one of the official languages of the first-century Roman Empire.

The good news is that God speaks the lingua franca of every place and age. Unless you have years to devote to learning multiple new languages, however, the odds are high that when you come to the Bible, you'll be reading a translation of words first spoken in someone else's native tongue. There are a number of factors involved in moving thoughts from one language to another that make translation challenging—especially when at least one of the languages involved is ancient.

First, the vocabularies of different languages never overlap precisely. The Georgian language usefully has a word for when you keep on eating despite being stuffed to explosion. In English, somewhat surprisingly, we have no similar term for that familiar holiday sensation of helplessly consuming a second slice of pie after that third helping of turkey. The Greek language of the New Testament possesses different words for sexual love and for love in friendship and for the selfless love of humankind. Sadly, in English, we possess just one term to cover all these things—not to mention our love for puppies and the smell of a new car.

Second, languages are often full of idioms. An idiom is a combination of words that has taken on a distinctive meaning that native speakers of the language take for granted but that wouldn't be obvious to a non-native speaker who simply knows the words' individual definitions. We know what we mean when we say in English, "It's raining cats and dogs out there!" but a Japanese speaker might well wonder why we think pets are falling from the sky. Or I might complain, "Food at Disneyland costs an arm and a leg!" leaving a Swahili speaker baffled about why I'm trading limbs for churros. In the biblical language of Hebrew, a person "hot in the nostrils" is angry. A translator must decide whether to translate the words as they stand or to try to sum up the meaning, like "It's raining hard" or "Food at Disneyland is very expensive."

Gender presents a particular challenge in crossing languages, as various languages use gendered terms differently. Even within the same language, treatment can change over time. Just a generation ago, it was normal for English speakers to use the word *man* to speak generically of humans; today, upon hearing that a trait is "common to men," most assume that this trait—like beards—is common to half the population. On the other hand, when I yell "Hurry up, you guys!" my friends easily understand me as beckoning men and women both, despite there having been a time when *guys* was clearly a masculine indicator. When a biblical writer uses a term like *brothers* or *men*, translators of the Bible must try to determine whether in the writer's own language and context that word would have been heard as gendered (that is, exclusive to males) or as encompassing men and women both (as in the phrase "you guys").

None of these challenges are insurmountable, and in fact the vast majority of English translations are remarkably good at finding ways to address them and communicate the Bible's message clearly. It's important to recognize, however, that every translation is also an interpretation. The individual or group who translated any Bible has made decisions about what they think the authors were trying to say and how those ideas should best be conveyed in English. Understanding this can help us be a little more cautious about placing too much theological freight on a single English word or short phrase. However good and reliable the translation, there is always some element of distance between the word that we see in English and the word originally written. When reading a translation, meaning tends to become clearer and more reliable as we look at larger thought units, such as sentences and paragraphs.

The specific challenges of translation just named here account for many small differences between Bibles. But the biggest reason that translations of the Bible differ from each other is that translators have different overall philosophies on how best to move between languages. Some translations practice what is called "formal" or "word-for-word" equivalence, trying to stick as closely as possible to the original language's words, grammar, and syntax. The benefit to this approach is that you get the most literal possible picture of the original text. The downside is it can be quite difficult to understand in English. At the other end of the spectrum are "functional" or "thought-for-thought" translations, in which translators focus on trying to capture the author's concept or idea in ways we would normally say it in English. These translations are willing to make some sacrifices in the literalness of individual words in order to provide greater clarity on the meaning of the author's whole thought.

Every Bible lands somewhere on this spectrum between formal and functional equivalence, and there is no single right or wrong place to be. The best Bible for you will depend in part on your needs as a reader. A literal translation can be useful if you're digging in for serious study. A functional translation might help the Bible feel more accessible. For readers who are new to the Bible, it's a good idea to start somewhere in the middle. The Common English Bible (CEB) is a strong midrange translation that I recommend, but the New International Version (NIV) and New Revised Standard Version (NRSV) are other popular midrange options.

If you are interested in discovering where your own current Bible falls along the translation spectrum, a quick online search of the phrase "Bible translation chart" will bring up many diagrams that will help you locate the most popular English Bibles according to their translation philosophy. If you've been reading the Bible for a long time, one of the best ways to refresh your reading is to try a new translation—especially one from a different part of the spectrum than where you're accustomed to reading.

8

THE STORY
Act 1, The Old Testament

One strange fact about the Bible's final form is that the sixty-six books that together compose its story do not appear in historical order. This means that reading the Bible cover to cover can sometimes feel like listening to an audiobook on shuffle. To make matters even more complicated, these sixty-six books encompass a variety of literary genres. It's as if you picked up a library book that moves, without warning, from romance to historical record to legal code to poetry.

This unusual combination of differing tones and writing conventions can make it difficult to see how the various parts of the Bible connect with each other or to pick out the story's broader plotline. Much like reading the CliffsNotes on *The Iliad* before tackling the book, starting out with some sort of picture of the Bible's larger story can help you begin to make out how seemingly disparate pages interact to form a coherent whole.[1] One way to summarize the story might go something like this . . .

* * * * *

In the beginning, God designed the world for beauty, order, and sheer joy. We humans were in some way formed unique among creation—shaped in God's image, given a special spark of God's creativity, God's freedom, God's powers of influence. We were made for relationship—for long laughter-filled dinners with each other and for sunset walks through the garden with God, talking through the complexities of love and of fully human existence. We were also assigned a job—to serve as God's "authorized representatives" to the rest of the world, cultivating the goodness of creation, helping call everything into the fullness of its God-intended life.[2]

But being created in God's image is a bit like being an infant born in the image of your parents: the DNA is there from the start, all the necessary building blocks of robust and mature likeness, but the journey isn't complete on day one. Through the process of moving through the world in companionship with God and of practicing our assigned vocation, we were meant to keep on growing up. We were intended to develop over time toward maturity, each day the resemblance to our divine Maker becoming a little bit stronger.

But instead of growing up, we humans went rogue. We exercised our God-given power and freedom against God's wise design. We began to duck God's calls and hide from the One we were meant to depend on for guidance. Therefore, instead of growing gradually clearer, the divine resemblance became distorted. It turned out that on our own, cut off from relationship with God, the power that remained in the fractured divine image was only enough for us drag the rest of creation down with us as we collapsed.

The land was ravaged by famine. Men used their strength to dominate women. Human life was bought and sold.

Vibrant species went extinct. People were lonely in a crowd. In a frenzy of fear and greed, we tore creation apart.

But despite all this pain and chaos, God decided the world was worth fighting for. So God devised a plan to save us from ourselves and win creation back to its intended, good design. That plan begins to unfold with a man named Abraham.

Stage one of the plan is simple: God will choose one ordinary person with all the normal human flaws. God will move through the world with him—talk to him, bless him, listen to him, slowly win his trust. And little by little, God will teach this one person what humanity had never truly understood: how to enjoy friendship with God, and how to participate in God's work of blessing and cultivating all the world.

In stage two of the plan, this one person, Abraham, will teach his family what he has learned from God about how to be truly, fully human. His children will come to meet God for themselves and learn their God-given vocation. They in turn will teach their own children, and all this will culminate in stage three, when Abraham's family will become a living, breathing billboard situated along the global highway, revealing God's true design: "Look here! This is the generous God you've been missing! This is the life you were meant for!"

This was the plan in motion. When Abraham's family, who call themselves the Israelites, are enslaved by the empire of Egypt, God breaks them out of slavery with dramatic plagues. This is essentially God's way of formally introducing God's self to the world: "Hi, my name is Yahweh"—this was the name God gave them—"I'm the God who hears the cries of the oppressed and delivers them." This is our first glimpse of a major theme that will return again and again in the Bible's story—God has a thing for rescuing people who cannot help themselves.

God offers the newly saved family of Israel a plot of earth, a place where they can live and follow God's lead and model for everyone else God's vision for what the world can be. God gives them a set of laws, a kind of "family code," if you will, to jump-start their imagination for what it might look like to live a more beautiful, fully human life under the direction of their Rescuer.

There's just one problem: the family chosen for the mission of being God's walking advertisement is just as broken and confused as all the other families on earth. They don't aspire to stand out as something radically new and alternative; they simply want to fit in. They want a piece of the forbidden fruit pie their neighbors are consuming. They'd prefer to pile up God's blessings like a dragon with its hoard, not be asked to spend their days giving those gifts away to other people.

The Israelites conquer their way into the land of Canaan, killing some inhabitants and displacing others on their way to claiming it. Then they settle in next to their new neighbors and get on with becoming exactly like everybody else. Each time they turn their backs on God and the mission they were meant for, things seem to fall apart. Then someone will say, "Hey, remember that God who rescued us that time?" The whole family will cry out to God for help, and God will send a leader (called a "judge") to get them out of their jam. But as soon as the crisis passes, they go back to business as usual, and the cycle starts over again.

After centuries caught in this downward spiral, the family of Israel finally decides to get really honest: they don't actually want to be a collection of people bound together by allegiance to the dreams of God; they just want to be a normal nation. They want the safety of an army, not God's promise of protection. They want a human leader to follow—preferably one who's tall and handsome—not an invisible being sitting on an invisible throne. They want a ruler to guard their borders and be on their side against everyone else, not a God who has a plan to care even for their enemies. The family of Israel bands together and demands that God give them a king.

To be clear, this was not the plan that God had in mind. This family was chosen to model God's more beautiful design for creation, not to emulate global distortions. But God honors the decisions of those made in God's own image. After all, there's no way to grow up when there are no real choices or consequences. And so, when the Israelites insist—despite God's warnings—God finally gives them what they asked for: a ruler like the rest.

Just as God had warned them, this experiment doesn't turn out well. Three kings into the new monarchy, the country erupts into conflict and splits in half, with a kingdom now called Israel to the north and a kingdom called Judah to the south. The two nations war with each other. The rich get richer and the poor get poorer. Some gain power. Others are enslaved. Enemies are slaughtered. The land is torn. The courts miscarry justice. Instead of introducing their neighbors to a God who desires to bless, the Israelites get in the habit of proclaiming a vengeful God who, truth be told, likes no one but them.

Amid all this chaos, a group of people arise called the prophets. A prophet is a person whose job is to speak on behalf of God. The prophets remind Israel of the reason God chose their family to start with, and point them back toward God's beautiful vision that they were meant to represent. They warn the Israelites, and especially their leaders, that if they persist in ignoring their divinely given mission, they'll eventually lose the gifts of land and protection that God had provided as equipment for living that mission out.

But the people of Israel and Judah refuse to revisit their purpose. They persist in imitating the same fear, greed, and violence that has the whole world in its grip. As a result, what the prophets predicted finally occurs. In 722 BCE, the empire of Assyria crushes the northern kingdom of Israel. The prophets tell Judah in the south that there's still time to re-commit to God's vision and avoid their sibling's fate. But in 586 BCE Judah finally falls as well, conquered by the empire of Babylon. The temple where they worshiped, their center of government, the whole nation they took so much pride in—all is destroyed, and the leaders of Judah are sent into exile. All the gold and all the glory for which they'd traded God's dreams are scattered into dust.

As is often the case with humans, losing everything pro-vokes some real soul-searching about where exactly things went wrong. The people finally begin to turn toward God again. Eventually, the exiles are permitted to return home and start rebuilding their lives. But there is no truly going back. The Israelites are now dominated by larger foreign powers, much as they'd been back in Egypt. They begin to wonder if they've used up the last of their chances. Some dream of a political savior who will get them back on track—by which they mean get them back to the glory days when they were a free nation with a real king of their own.

By the end of the Old Testament, it is evident that even after many centuries, the family chosen for the mission of modeling God's alternative plan for the world has still largely failed to catch the vision. Even their dreams have been caught up in the universal distortions.

9

THE STORY
Act 2, The New Testament

But then the story takes a turn that nobody saw coming—even though there were subtle hints along the way that this was always God's intent, the only true solution to the global chaos: God decides that the only way to get the message through correctly is to deliver it God's self.

This approach of coming in person offers a chance to finally correct all the misperceptions that have proliferated through the years, all the terrible misapprehensions of who God really is. God can introduce God's self to the world first-hand, explain what it is that God has always longed for. But that isn't all. By coming into the world as a part of the people of Israel, God can also take up the task entrusted to Abraham's family—live the truly human life, model the true design, execute the mission of blessing every piece of the broken world.

So God enters the world as a man named Jesus—fully God and also fully Israel, humanity as humans were always meant to be. And God-in-human-flesh rather quietly begins to foment global revolution.

It starts with a simple message: the world as you see it isn't as it's meant to be. In fact, it's broken in every part. But

God is on a mission to bring the true design back—a new, vibrant creation Jesus describes as "the kingdom of God." The kingdom of God is something so much bigger than another human-nation-like-the-others that Israel once settled for. This is a whole, entire, borderless world come truly alive under the rule of God.

To be sure the picture is clear, Jesus offers demonstrations of God's more beautiful vision. He brings raging weather under control. He gives food to those who lack it and challenges those who have too much to give up their excess. He heals broken bodies and broken hearts. He draws outsiders into community. He empowers women. He teaches God's concern for birds and flowers. He brings enemies together and calls them family. He names ordinary people friends and confidantes of God. And everywhere he goes, Jesus says the same thing: "God is so much closer than you think, and a new world is breaking in. Now is your chance to get on board and transfer your citizenship."

Many people are amazed and drawn to what they see in Jesus, irresistibly attracted to the picture of the new world that he casts. But in every system, there are some who profit from the corrupt status quo. There are also many others who prefer familiar brokenness to a change they can't control. These decide they'd prefer the old world order, thank you. And they plot together to kill Jesus to shut him up.

It would be easy to blame these local leaders for what happens to Jesus. After all, they act to guard their own social privilege, or their excessive certainty about what God desires. But these leaders don't act alone. They are abetted by a mob of ordinary people who lash out reactively to rumors that stoke their darkest fears and fantasies. The man in charge of

Jesus' trial chooses popularity over truth. The soldiers who nail Jesus to a cross, the Roman Empire's preferred method of criminal enforcement, go through the motions of their jobs without asking what role they are playing in maintaining an unjust system.

Jesus' own followers don't perform any better than anybody else. One justifies betrayal in order to line his pocketbook. Another comes out swinging a sword in Jesus' defense, perpetuating the cycle of violence Jesus preached against. Some flee when they get scared. When the cost of following Jesus' lead suddenly seems too high, one disciple denies knowing Jesus at all.

The trouble with the world, it appears, is that every single person has come down with a deadly infection known as sin. Hidden anxieties and little selfish ambitions ricochet off each other, leaving destruction in their wake. The greatest atrocity in history, the crucifixion of God incarnate, is not inflicted by some super-villain or monster with scales and fangs. It is an agonizing death of a thousand poisoned paper cuts, inflicted by a thousand different, ordinary human hands.

We humans, in our soul distortion, together torture and kill our own Creator, who was only in the world to save us from ourselves. This is rock bottom, as bad as it gets. But something happens next that is hard to explain. The biblical writers stammer trying to wrap words around it.

On the cross, at this execution of Jesus—in this moment, all the world-rending chaos we humans unleashed finally lands in one giant tidal wave. All the greed and violence, fear and selfishness, pride and hate and deceit, all of it has added up to this: the very murder of God. But as he hangs there dying, Jesus takes it all. He soaks up all the blood and tears and fears and mistakes into his own body. The worst humans could do, the worst we could think of, all the darkness and pain we unleashed on the world, Jesus draws it all into himself. Jesus takes even evil and death itself and pulls them into the center of God.

God's judgment falls on all this evil and shatters it, like marble striking glass. All our mistakes are swept away like leaves in a rushing current. The darkness meets God's light and vanishes like mist. The life of God is just too strong for the death and chaos to withstand it. Three days after he is killed, Jesus walks back out of his grave, and he carries the rest of the world with him.

On the surface, many things look the same on the far side of resurrection. The world has not been instantly transformed into all it was meant to be. But beneath the surface, something at the heart of things has changed. The death grip of evil has been broken; its claim over us is gone. A new story has been opened; a set of choices exist that were not there before. The reset button has been pressed; tomorrow doesn't have to look the same as yesterday.

Jesus tells his followers after his resurrection that this next chapter of history will be unlike anything before. God is starting a new world right in the middle of the old, broken one. This new world will finally reflect the true shape of God's design from the start. This new world is under the rule of Jesus, and he will sign citizenship papers for anyone who offers him their allegiance.

To those who choose to join his new world, Jesus gives a gift called the Holy Spirit—a deposit on better things still to come. Just as Jesus was God in one human body, the Spirit is God's presence within the bodies of the whole community of those who offer Jesus their allegiance. The Spirit throws open the communication lines with God so we can talk and listen. The Spirit takes up the work of untangling the distortions in that spark of divine image so we can finally grow toward maturity. The Spirit empowers Jesus' followers to at last take up our true human vocation: becoming his apprentices, nurturing creation, and carrying God's blessing to the farthest ends of the globe.

Jesus' apprentices, the people who choose to join his new world, have a name. The Bible calls them the church. This collective of people who have bound themselves to Jesus are instructed to take up the mission first entrusted to Abraham's family. The church is a gathering of God's people together living out God's alternative vision for the world, a way of life so beautiful it makes the neighbors say, "I want some of that!"

The people of Jesus don't get to write the story's final pages. The end of the Bible makes it clear that only God can act to clear away the rubble of the old world and finally usher in an age when the new world is all there is. God has promised that someday God will do this—sooner than we think. But in the meantime, the people of Jesus witness to what is still coming. Their life together is meant to be a preview of coming attractions. We who choose Jesus live under the new world order now as a sign of the goodness that's in store for everything. We relate to God as we were meant to from the start—in constant, intimate communication. We take up our vocation of cultivating creation, tending the flourishing of every part. And in doing this, we keep growing up into the image of our Maker, beginning the work now that will be ours forever—always maturing more and more into a fuller likeness of the beauty of God.

The Bible's layered and complex nature means there is more than one way to tell its story well. Different tellings might emphasize different key themes or trace different core threads. But for me, this is what emerges from the rest as the very heart of the story: a new world that is rising, just over the horizon, and a people who are living in the first light of dawn.

10

DINING WITH STRANGERS
A Posture for Reading

ave you ever gone to a party in a terrible mood, convinced that the conversation will be boring, the music selection appalling, the food atrocious, the entire evening a colossal waste of time? Then perhaps you've noticed that, for better or worse, experience has a funny way of conforming itself to expectation. Primed for enjoyment, we generally find a reason to laugh. Primed for outrage, we generally find cause for that too. Enter into conversation assuming the worst about someone, and you are almost certain to find evidence confirming your suspicions the moment they open their mouth. The truth is, in approaching the Bible—much like everything else in life—the outcome often depends significantly on your posture going in.

One of the challenges of reading the Bible at this time in the West is that many of us have been educated to read from a default posture of critique. We are taught to approach literature with what's been described as a "hermeneutics of suspicion."[1] We have learned to break texts apart, look for concealed motives and problems, respond first with observation of all that may be wrong.[2] Faced with an ancient religious text like the Bible, many modern readers find their finely honed critical instincts triggered all at once. Book of Joshua—no loving God would ever command the slaughter of cities! Jonah—are we really supposed to believe this guy was yakked up by a fish?! Revelation's "whore of Babylon"— yet another regressive gender stereotype.

Let's be fair to ourselves and each other—there are vital questions to be asked on all these fronts, questions about how our holy texts form us and toward what, questions of how we communicate without perpetuating cycles of harm, questions even of how we understand the core character of God. There are questions of faith, and questions of practice, worthy of careful consideration. We are not wrong to ask them.

But it's also the case that sometimes, as modern people, we get stuck in a mode of deconstruction. We can even develop a kind of addiction to the thrill of tearing things apart. Legitimate questions of faith and faithfulness become like a detective's interrogation. The Bible is a suspect, handcuffed to a chair. We shine a flashlight in its eyes and demand, "Explain yourself!" We throw out questions rapid-fire in hopes of tripping it up, catching it in an inconsistent statement.

In the midst of such procedures, we often tell ourselves that ours is a crusade of justice and truth. But if we are honest, we might also be forced to acknowledge that we prefer a bolted-down table and a bit of skepticism fixed between us and Scripture. The beauty of interrogation is that it's a one-directional exercise. It keeps us in control, feeling superior to the rest. It ensures there's always one more question between us and the need to answer for our own lives. It's much easier to make our way through the world comfortably when no one has the authority to challenge us or talk back.

But while questions are healthy and important, our relationship with the Bible was never meant to be a one-sided interrogation. The most important thing we may ever do is suspend our questions for awhile and relinquish the seat of power, put ourselves on the other side of the table for a change. Because if we have questions for Scripture, it also has questions for us. Book of Joshua—How are you and your people (political party, religious tradition, or informal online "tribe") behaving toward your enemies? Does that behavior reflect the character of the God revealed in Jesus? Jonah—Are you offering others as lavish a grace as you yourself depend on? Revelation—Where are you being seduced by the siren song of consumerism or nationalism and overlooking the deadly spiritual cost?

Scripture can take our hardest questions; the Bible isn't intimidated. But it's critical that we don't stop, that we don't close the cover, until we've allowed our own lives to be questioned with the same rigor we've applied. The Bible unveils its power most fully to the one who lets it have its turn leading the dialogue. The most revolutionary truth the Bible may teach modern people is this: you are suspect yourself.

In a way, relationship with the Bible is much like interacting with a stranger from another country. If I take everything that stranger says and does and immediately run it through the filter of my own prior assumptions, I learn nothing. When we enter any relationship with a starting posture of suspicion and hostility, it becomes difficult to truly hear what the other person has to say. Instead of receiving from another a deeper understanding of ourselves and the world, we are deafened by the clamor of our own rebounding judgments.

It is no coincidence that one of the Bible's prominent ethical teachings is about hospitality to the stranger and the foreigner. In Genesis 18, Abraham (the father of biblical faith) spots three strangers near his home and rushes out to greet them. At some point in the midst of grilling the steaks, Abraham discovers he is actually playing host to God. The Bible often comes to us much like this: a stranger on the road whose accent seems foreign, whose unfamiliar customs trigger an impulse for dismissal. But beneath the ancient Palestinian garb that seems so strange to us, it may well be God who is visiting us.

To receive a stranger well requires humility, an openness to being challenged, a willingness to consider the possibility that our prior assumptions might not be correct. It requires a hopeful expectation that the other may have something to teach us precisely in their otherness. It may be that the Bible's distance, it's very "foreignness," is a crucial part of the message—a holy, humbling disruption of our undisclosed distortions and our unanchored certainties.

A posture of hospitality rather than hostility or suspicion is one crucial factor in whether we are able to make out the voice of God speaking in Scripture. A second and perhaps more surprising factor that affects what we will hear is what we plan to do after we close the cover.

Some subjects lend themselves well to abstract learning. My ability to understand geometry is little affected by whether the grilled cheese sandwich I ate last night was cut into trapezoids. But there are other forms of knowledge that are difficult to acquire except in actual practice. People preparing to get married, or to become parents, or even just to downhill ski find themselves recipients of many well-meaning words of wisdom (at least a few of which are actually true). But that wisdom often becomes truly meaningful only over time, in the context of lived experience.

The principle of practice preceding comprehension is never truer than when it comes to complex matters of God and the human soul. Some readers attempt to sit at a neutral distance and "solve" the Bible like an algebra equation that can be decoded with the proper application of known principles. But trying to comprehend Scripture without integrating it into lived practice is like trying to learn how to ski without ever leaving the lodge.

The only way to truly comprehend the Bible's message is to begin with obedience. For many of us, this seems counterintuitive. We prefer to imagine a process of learning that works more like this: (1) figure out what every word of the Bible means and exactly why God commands what God does; and (2) *then* decide if it's reasonable to actually walk this stuff out. But in actual fact, the process of gaining knowledge often works more like this: (1) throw yourself into the Bible's wild story and live as if it were true; and (2) *then* begin to discover in practice why God says the things God does and what profound truths the Bible has always been gesturing toward.

The Bible is not a mathematics textbook but a guide to the oceans of God. If you truly want to understand what it is teaching about God, about the world, about the shape of the fully human life, there is only one way to do it: by getting wet. You begin by simply gathering up the bits of knowledge that you have and heading out into the water. You act. You practice the strokes as the Bible outlines them. You swim out as far as you dare. You come back to shore, read the book's pages again, and this time, with salt on your skin, hear them a little differently. Then you head back to the water and swim some more. Sometimes it's only after deep-sea diving a dozen times that the descriptions begin to make sense. Sometimes the activity leads, and then the comprehension follows.

It's certainly possible to learn techniques that will help us hear the Bible more clearly. But the most determinant factor in how well you'll ultimately comprehend its message is how much you are willing to engage, to experiment, to put skin in the game. Those who swim in the shallows will learn something real. Those who risk the depths will learn more.

You can count on this: there is no one in the world whom God is more eager to talk to than the one who fully intends to go out and do something about what they hear. At the end of the day, God is looking not for sideline observers but for actual dance partners. The Bible sets the music. God's Spirit will teach the moves. But if you want to learn the art of dancing, you have to be willing to get out on the floor.

STORYTIME

Unwrapping the Book of Jonah

"AM I REALLY supposed to believe a big fish swallowed Jonah?"

This is one of the questions about the Bible I am asked most frequently. To some, Jonah's story is emblematic of so many stories in the Bible that seem wildly improbable. Ax heads floating? Bread multiplying? The dead walking out of their graves? Can a thinking modern person really be expected to take such tales seriously?

Before I reply, let me tell you a story.

* * * * *

There once was a guy named Jonah, whom God called to be a prophet. His job was pretty straightforward: go to the city of Nineveh, home of his nation's most ruthless enemies, and tell the people there that God was displeased with their bad behavior. "Sure thing, God," Jonah says. Then he goes to the local port and gets on the first ship he can find—sailing in the opposite direction.

God sends a storm to rattle the ship, and all the poor pagan sailors get on their knees and pray to their idols for rescue. Who is the only person on the ship who doesn't show up to the prayer meeting? Jonah, representative of the one true and living God. Good old Jonah is down below deck, giving his God the silent treatment.

With classic maritime superstition, the sailors roll the dice to see who's to blame for the storm. Even the dice know that this is on Jonah. When brought up on deck and questioned, Jonah responds unapologetically, "Well, yes, I am in fact a worshiper of the one true God of the sea, whom (I maybe should have clarified earlier?) I'm currently on the run from."

It's during this conversation that it finally begins to dawn on Jonah that it could maybe have been a bit of a jerk move to implicate a boat full of innocent people when he chose to pick a fight with God. When it seems evident they're all likely to go under, Jonah suggests that the sailors save themselves by tossing him overboard. It isn't exactly the happy ending he was hoping for, but hey, look on the bright side—at least he won't have to go on that stupid mission of God's.

The pagan sailors, though terrified of the storm, fear Jonah's God too much to threaten his life. This is, of course, deeply ironic, since Jonah has apparently feared his own God too little to concern himself. But when the storm does not die down, the sailors finally give in to the inevitable and do what Jonah has suggested, sending him down to Davy Jones's locker.

This is where the story of Jonah should reasonably end—with Jonah as fish food, as just punishment for open rebellion and reckless endangerment. But that isn't what happens. Instead, God has unaccountable mercy on this most pathetic of prophets, and sends a fish—that's right, a giant, ridiculously improbable fish—to swallow Jonah whole and carry him to safety.

For a couple of hours, Jonah is pretty jazzed about his miraculous escape from death. He even writes a hymn of praise to the wonderful, blessed, glorious God who saved his life despite his rebellion: "Salvation comes from the Lord!" he gushes.

After a days' long intensive worship songwriting session, Jonah is barfed back on land, and God comes to him a second time and says, "Now go preach to Nineveh." But Jonah's gratitude fades faster than the fish stench on his robes. It seems that God can in fact make Jonah go to Nineveh, but God can't make him be happy about it. Jonah shows up in Nineveh and preaches the most half-hearted sermon in homiletics history: "Listen, everybody: in forty days Nineveh will be overthrown. Now does anyone know where I can get a decent cup of coffee?"

The pitiful sermon is five words in Hebrew. Jonah conveniently "forgets" to mention that the message came from God and skips the altar call completely. But one sentence into the world's lamest sermon, the entire capital population of the evil empire falls to their knees in sorrow for their choices. And God decides to have mercy on them and not destroy them after all.

That's when the truth finally comes out. It turns out that *this* was Jonah's worst nightmare all along. He hadn't sailed off in the opposite direction because he was afraid of being beaten to death by the biker gangs of Nineveh. His real fear had always been that God would go all soft like this. "Isn't this what I said before I left home?" he rants. "I knew you'd get like this, God. You're always so stinking 'gracious and compassionate,' 'slow to anger,' and 'over-flowing with love,' constantly refraining from giving people what's coming to them. That's what I hate about you, God! Your freaking grace ruins everything!"

Jonah stomps out of the repentant city but decides to stay in view, because if God comes to God's senses and decides to fry those Ninevites like the little *#?&! ants they are, he doesn't want to miss the bonfire. He sits out in the desert under the scorching sun, all hot and furious and miserable but determined not to budge from his vigil of terror. God feels sorry yet again for the pitiful prophet and sends a fast-growing plant to give him a bit of shade. Naturally, Jonah is thrilled. But overnight a worm chews up the plant, and the next afternoon Jonah finds himself pouting under a shriveled stalk.

This is the final straw for Jonah. How dare God do this to him! How dare God kill his plant! God inquires curiously, "Do you think it's right for you to be this angry over the death of one small plant?"

"You're darn right it is," Jonah replies. "I'm so mad I wish I were dead."

God responds, "So just so I'm sure I have this straight: you're furious at me for killing a plant you spent twelve hours with—a plant, by the way, that I sent so you could spend yesterday pouting in comfort. But you don't think I should give a second thought to killing a giant city teeming with people too ignorant to even tell their right hand from their left, not to mention a whole lot of innocent animals as well?"

Here ends the story of Jonah.

* * * * *

So. Is the story of Jonah true?

The Bible is certainly full of tales that do not seem to comport with known natural laws. The ministry of Jesus is saturated with such stories—blind people seeing and lame people walking and vats of water turning into the finest wine.

For myself, I believe in the working laws of science, the principles we know of the world's staggeringly elegant design. But I also believe that history is full of occurrences for which no known law accounts. Live long enough and you might just find yourself witness to one of these happenings, something too strange to explain and too wonderful to deny.

I don't claim to have all the answers about these things, but there are a few things I feel confident about. First, what seems reasonable to believe depends in part on what you have experienced. Second, it would be rather arrogant for me to claim that because I haven't personally experienced something, it couldn't possibly be true. And third, in a world that is open to the presence of God, anything is possible. At the end of the day, this is the Bible's radical claim that every reader must grapple with: the door between heaven and earth stands open, and a whole lot of unexpected things can happen in the thin space between.[1]

But it's also possible in reading many of the Bible's stories to get sidetracked debating the details and miss the central point. What is the book of Jonah actually about? The fish, despite its prominence in children's picture books, turns out to be a relatively minor player. The self-consciously ridiculous improbability of the fish-belly rescue serves in this book only to drive home the unimaginable lengths to which God will go to show mercy to one bottom-dwelling, irrational sourpuss of a prophet.

The book of Jonah tells the story of a people (perhaps you have met them) who are swallowed, time and time again, by God's extravagant, inexplicable mercy—but who immediately forget their own story every time they touch the shore. It's the tale of a people who can't even smell the pungent grace still clinging to their clothes. It's the tale of a people whose very lives—just like the lives of their neighbors—hang on a precious thread at which they are constantly sawing away.

I don't know much about aquatic animal anatomy, but I can tell you for a fact that I've met Jonah personally: he often shows up in my mirror, staring back at me. When I'm really paying attention, I start to smell the fishy scent wafting off my sweater. Each time I read Jonah, I laugh and I cringe and I awaken to the truth of my own life. The question most central to the book of Jonah is not whether I can swallow the fish. The question is what Fish has swallowed me and whether I can allow that same Fish to swallow my enemies too.

PART II

LEARNING TO READ

11

GRABBING BUGGIES
Introduction to Interpretation

I don't believe in interpreting the Bible!" the outraged man sitting across from me insisted, after inquiring about the subject on which I was writing. "I just believe in reading the Bible and doing what it says!" This reaction isn't uncommon among longtime Bible readers. For many people, there is something viscerally alarming about the suggestion that relationship with the Bible should require any kind of interpretive step.

In my experience, this alarm is typically animated by two concerns. The first is the worry that if the Bible isn't accepted as sufficiently clear on its own, it could become functionally accessible only to educated religious "elites."[1] The majority of people could lose their sense of direct access to God. The second concern is the suspicion that "interpretation" might be just a code word for the intellectual gymnastics people do to avoid any truth that is simply inconvenient or difficult. The notion of interpretation seems to open the Bible up to all kinds of potential abuses, making the Bible sound rather like a "choose your own adventure" novel where the outcome is determined in large part by the reader's preferences.

These concerns aren't without cause. The history of Christianity contains too many examples of religious professionals bending texts to suit their own interests or those of the institutional status quo. There are also plenty of examples of untrained people who heard God speak in powerful, world-changing ways. Truth has never been the exclusive property of scholars and experts, and the Bible itself is full of stories of God showing up to talk precisely with those whom the system has deemed unfit (see Luke 1:5-38 for an excellent case study).

It is also true that all of us are guilty at times of looking for ways to avoid the obvious implications of straightforward but challenging texts. Take Jesus' command "Love your enemies*" (Matthew 5:44). Many readers spend far more time inventing possible asterisked exception clauses to this command—"*All enemies except Osama bin Laden . . . and Great-Aunt Mildred . . . and that punk who keyed my new car . . . because, you know, *evil*, man!"—than asking what they would do if Jesus actually meant what he said.

But despite these reasons to exercise caution, there is no way to avoid interpretation as a necessary aspect of communication. We engage in interpretation all the time, in virtually every interaction we have during the day, usually without even noticing what we are doing. When my friend and I enter a store together and she asks me to grab her a "buggy," I instinctively picture a black covered cart being pulled by a horse. This picture jumps to mind because I regularly visit places in the rural Midwest where I'm likely to see Amish people driving such vehicles down back roads. However, because my friend grew up in New England, when *she* says the word *buggy*, she is picturing a metal shopping cart like you use to wheel around groceries. I might waste the rest of my day pointlessly seeking a man about a horse unless I draw on my knowledge of my friend's background to help me properly decipher what she's really asking for.

At the most basic level, biblical interpretation is about making sure I'm not reaching for a horse and carriage when God wants a shopping cart. We approach the Bible as authorized eavesdroppers. We are intended by God to listen in, but we are also tuning in on words first spoken to someone else—someone who had their own language and background and associations. When we interpret, we are trying to match our mental images as much as possible with those of the original recipients of the words. In effect, this means that when Luke describes Jesus sleeping in a "boat," I want to be imagining a small, wooden fishing vessel like they had in the first century, not a three-level luxury yacht parked in a California bay.

Far from imposing my own preferred meaning on the text, interpretation actually aims at the opposite. Good interpretation helps me recognize where I might be accidentally imposing ideas that are foreign to the text. It prevents my reading of the Bible from turning into an inkblot test that reveals more about me and my personal proclivities than it does about God and God's desires.

Opening the Bible is a little bit like walking into a room in which a group of people are in the middle of a passionate discussion. God and the people of faith before us were engaged in a centuries-long conversation that has been captured on the pages of the Bible. We are meant to join in that conversation. But before we jump in, we'd do well to figure out what everyone else is talking about. Otherwise we might walk into the room to hear the words "My battery is dead" and whip out our jumper cables, never realizing that God and our ancestors were discussing watches. To be clear: there's no virtue in revving the engine when God is pointing to our wrist. Interpretation involves hearing as clearly as possible what the other parties are saying so that we are in a position to respond appropriately.

So the first purpose of interpretation is to help us match our mental picture with that of the writers. But there is a second purpose as well: to expose what we ourselves are taking for granted when we assess the text's "plain meaning." Some readers suggest that when it comes to the Bible, their goal is just to read the "plain sense" of what the text says. This goal seems sensible, even admirable. It is precisely the idea the Protestant reformers had during the Reformation, which radically reshaped Christianity in the 1500s. The reformers believed that if they could just disentangle the Bible from the centuries' worth of past interpretations and translate it into the language of the common people, everyone would finally be free to read the Bible for themselves and see what it really said. They assumed that without interpretation clouding the view, the true meaning would be plain and obvious to everyone who read it.

To their dismay, the reformers quickly discovered that this was not the case. Different social locations, national identities, personal experiences, and starting questions caused readers to perceive the "plain sense" of the text very differently.[2] Even the reformers themselves drew different conclusions from each other. Those differences are still playing out in many kinds of Christian churches that exist today.

One example of how reader assumptions can vary can be found in reflection on 2 Samuel 11. This chapter tells the story of King David and Bathsheba, a married woman whom David spots bathing while strolling on his palace roof and with whom he then has an affair. More than one reader of this story has implicated Bathsheba in a deliberate act of seduction, suggesting that she basically fan-girled David, deliberately exposing herself to his view in order to catch the royal's eye. To other readers, however, the story could suggest a happily married woman who was coerced, even raped, by a powerful man whom she could not resist without fear for her life. Given that David ends up killing her husband, such a fear is not entirely unwarranted. Which version of this story strikes you as the "plain sense" of things may say more about your own social location or personal experiences than it does about the text itself. What we see, what we hear, what we read between the lines of the Bible's stories often depends on where we ourselves stand in the world.

This simple reality—that our experiences inform our perception—explains why it is important to consider what we are taking for granted when we consider a text's "obvious" meaning. The goal is not to read the Bible naked (so to speak), with all our assumptions and experiences totally stripped away. Frankly, that would be impossible. There is no such thing as a fully "neutral" reader; we cannot help but be shaped by the time and place in which we live.

Yet learning to recognize the impact of our own experiences and identities on how we are reading is another step toward making sure that we are seeing more than a reflection of ourselves in the text. It allows us to take into account the possible gap between the assumptions and experiences that we've brought to the biblical text, and the assumptions and experiences that the original hearers might have brought, coming as they did from a world with more donkeys and fewer drones. When we come to the Bible, we pause to identify what lenses we are wearing and to ask how they may be coloring our view. To bring the story into focus, it may be necessary to deliberately substitute our own lenses for a set more closely matched with those of the original audience.[3]

You might say interpretation is a key act of respect that we owe every communication partner, human or divine. It is an attempt to ensure that we are hearing as clearly as possible the voice that is speaking to us and not simply the reverberating echo of our own thoughts.

12

SPLICED
Literary Context

In 1995 a movie was released called *Se7en*. Its promoters ran an ad with a quotation from *Entertainment Weekly* declaring the movie "a small masterpiece." Sounds like a winner, right? But anyone who took the time to look up the full review would have discovered that it actually read, "The credit sequence, with its jumpy frames and near-subliminal flashes of psychoparaphernalia, is a small masterpiece of dementia."[1]

When we sit down in front of virtually any passage in the Bible, there are two fundamental interpretive questions we can ask that will go a long way toward ensuring that we hear its message as clearly as possible. The first question requires no specialized knowledge or outside tools to answer, yet simply paying attention to it can improve our understanding of many parts of the Bible. The question is this: How does the passage I'm reading relate to what comes immediately before and after it? The answer to this question is what's known as the passage's literary context.

Imagine pulling a novel off a library shelf and flipping it open at random to find a couple rushing down a grocery store aisle, frantically shoveling food and toilet paper into a cart. What might you assume is going on? Well, if you're a resident of a coastal city and it happens to be summer, odds are good your mind might jump straight to preparations for a hurricane. But if you flip back a couple of pages in the book, you might well discover that something entirely different is unfolding. Maybe instead of a hurricane, they're actually facing an impending North Dakota blizzard. Or maybe they're teenagers grabbing Red Vines and Mountain Dew on their way to TP someone's house, or they're in a hurry because they are robbing the store while their friend flirts with the clerk. The surrounding context of the story helps you understand the couple's actions on this particular page in the proper light.

Most of us have probably seen examples in the media where a line from a politician's speech is extracted by an opponent and applied in an attack ad in a way that is totally foreign to the intent of the original speech. When we see this happen to a candidate we support, we find it maddening. "He might have said those words," we protest, "but that isn't what he meant!"

This kind of thing happens all the time when it comes to the Bible, often without anyone even noticing. We take a single sentence or paragraph, disconnect it from the larger passage where it appears, and use it in ways that have little to do with its meaning in its original context. Even where the words are technically correct, they can be used to speak falsely. This is why the most basic and also most important step in biblical interpretation is simply to make sure we are reading each text in light of what appears around it.

A good example of the difference literary context makes is Psalm 51. Verses 16-17 read,

You don't want sacrifices.

> If I gave an entirely burned offering,
>> you wouldn't be pleased.
> A broken spirit is my sacrifice, God.
>> You won't despise a heart, God, that is broken and
>> crushed.

Reading this passage on its own like this, removed from its place in the whole chapter, the meaning might seem obvious: "I guess God doesn't actually care about sacrifices or offerings. Great! I'll save my money for bathing in pumpkin spice lattes." However, if you read just two verses further into the psalm, you would find that the author goes on to say,

> Then you will again want sacrifices of righteousness—
>> entirely burned offerings and complete offerings.
> Then bulls will again be sacrificed on your altar.

When the literary context is taken into account, it becomes clear that the writer of Psalm 51 never meant to imply that God is indifferent to offerings. Instead, the psalmist was actually arguing that offerings and sacrifices only matter when the heart behind them is right. Otherwise, they're simply empty gestures, like moving your arm in and out of the chip bowl to drive up the step count on your Fitbit. If you don't read the whole page, you might well miss the point and misinterpret the Bible's message.

In Mark 12:41-44, Jesus and his disciples are in the temple, their place of worship, watching an impoverished woman put her very last pennies into the offering plate. Jesus turns to his disciples and says,

I assure you that this poor widow has put in more than everyone who's been putting money in the treasury. All of them are giving out of their spare change. But she from her hopeless poverty has given everything she had, even what she needed to live on.

Read on its own, removed from its literary context, this story sounds for all the world like a straightforward object lesson in radical generosity: if only more people would be like the widow, who gave all she had to her religious community! However, if you pay careful attention to what appears around this story, Jesus' observation about the widow becomes more complicated. Just before pointing out the widow to his followers, in Mark 12:38-40, Jesus says,

Watch out for the legal experts. They like to walk around in long robes. They want to be greeted with honor in the markets. They long for places of honor in the synagogues and at banquets. They are the ones who *cheat widows out of their homes*, and to show off they say long prayers. They will be judged most harshly. (emphasis mine)

Notice that in this statement, Jesus critiques the religious leadership of his day and specifically accuses them of cheating widows—the very sort of impoverished person whom he is about to make the center of attention.

Now look at what happens in the story immediately after Jesus' encounter with the widow. In Mark 13:1-2, on their way out of the temple after seeing the widow, the disciples speak admiringly of the enormous stones and buildings that make up the temple complex—symbols of the religious system which the woman's offering supports. Instead of marveling with them over the grandeur of the architecture, Jesus replies, "Do you see these enormous buildings? Not even one stone will be left upon another. All will be demolished."

The story of the widow's offering in the book of Mark is sandwiched between a statement indicting religious leaders for robbing widows and a prediction of the destruction of religious space. While this poor woman does indeed have much to teach in her example of radical faith and generosity, within the literary context it also becomes clear that for Jesus, her story is also a challenge to the religious status quo of his day. It raises many complex questions: Why does this widow only have two pennies? What is the reason for her "hopeless poverty"? What exactly is the relationship between this dazzling religious system and this invisible woman whose plight apparently no one but Jesus has even noticed?

In one sense, applying the principle of literary context is rather simple. Before interpreting a passage, you simply check what happens immediately before and immediately after it. You might look for key words or concepts that tie the sections together. For example, the repetition of words—*widow* in Mark 12; *sacrifice* in Psalm 51—is often a tip-off as to how stories or poetic lines are connected. Connecting words like *however* and *therefore* are also important indicators that an argument is developing in which each point depends in some way on the point before. When you see connecting words (*therefore*) or carryover images (*widow*), it's one clue to slow down and ask how the sections relate to or illuminate each other.

But the tricky part of attending to literary context is that there is no strict rule of how wide a net to cast. Reading the sentences that immediately surround a particular passage can provide a useful starting place for making sure you understand what conversation the Bible means to provoke. In many cases, a line or paragraph takes on even more layers of meaning when you read it in the context of the book as a whole. Paul's declaration in Philippians 4:11—that he has "learned how to be content in any circumstance"—takes on a whole different resonance when you read the beginning of his letter and learn that he's not sipping drinks with umbrellas in a Mediterranean villa, but rather sitting in prison, wrapped in chains, contemplating his own possible execution. In narrative sections of the Bible, a single person's character may be developed over several chapters. Attending to literary context might include stepping back slightly to consider the significance of a particular event in light of the larger story.

As every photographer knows, snapshots can reveal truth, but they can also be deceiving. Sometimes the critical information for properly understanding the scene lies just beyond the frame. Not everything is as it appears at first glance. Attending to literary context means always reading with our peripheral vision open, attuned to the possible significance of the scene unfolding *around* the current object of our focus. The wider our scan, the more information we can factor in that may be relevant to the conclusions we draw.[2]

13

SEA CHANGE
Historical Context

"W hy does God hate water?" a woman asked me with concern. She was the proud owner of a beachfront house, and the lapping of ocean waves was the most peaceful sound she knew. But that afternoon she'd read Revelation 21:1, which states that at the end of time, when God finally banishes evil and sets the whole world right, there will no longer be any sea. For what possible reason, she wondered, was God plotting to eliminate her favorite part of creation?

For many people today, the idea of "the sea" conjures visions of sunbathing and sandcastles, or maybe the soothing sound of sleep machines. But for the world of the Bible, the sea represented something else entirely. To ancient people, the sea was a symbol of chaos, disorder, and even evil. In the Mediterranean region, storms swept up suddenly and powerfully, and shipwrecks were both common and deadly. Therefore, when the book of Revelation declares that there will not be any sea in the world God sets right, it isn't implying a divine distaste for water or for restful days at the beach. Instead, Revelation paints a picture of a world in which threats have been eliminated—a world that is finally, fully at peace.

John, the author of Revelation, was a first-century resident of a small Mediterranean island called Patmos. It's no surprise, then, that when John has a vision of the future, he sees a picture of the sea that is consistent with his own experience of water. God still has things to say to us through John's story, even many centuries and half a world away. But as we noted earlier, we are coming to the conversation in the position of authorized eavesdroppers. The starting terms of the conversation we are joining—the vocabulary, the images, the references—have already been primed to the original audience—in this case, John, who saw the visions, and the first-century communities to which he wrote.

After looking for the literary context, there is a second essential question we ask of every passage we interpret: What information about the text's own time and culture might help me better understand what it is describing? The answer to this question involves the text's historical context. When we explore historical context, we are trying to uncover the information that other participants in the biblical conversation—God, the human authors, and the original recipients of the book—are taking for granted because of the setting they shared.

Many readers of the Christmas story are mystified as to why the people of the little town of Bethlehem made Mary, the mother of Jesus, give birth in a stable and stick her baby in a manger. I mean, seriously—where's the human decency? Was there really nobody in this town who would give up their bed for a woman in labor? We are baffled by this detail because, when we read the Christmas story, most of us instinctively picture the sorts of houses and barns we have today. We imagine one building out front where the people and their potato chips live, another in the back for the cows and their hay. Mary is essentially left to give birth out in the garage.

However, a first-century Palestinian home was quite different from ours. Animals spent the night inside the house, both for their safety and to contribute needed body heat. The animals stayed in a slightly lowered part of the room, right beside the family's communal living area. A manger was often carved into the slightly higher living room floor. On that first Christmas Eve, in a small village where guest rooms were clogged with visiting out-of-towners, it appears that owners of an ancient house graciously offered Mary a place to give birth within their family's own (donkey-warmed) living space.[1]

When we fail to ask the question of historical context, by default we typically insert assumptions based on our own time and context. We try to paint the picture, but we get crucial details wrong. Sometimes, as in the case of Jesus' birthplace, not much damage is done (aside from some minor aspersions cast on the character of the noble citizens of Bethlehem). But other times, neglecting historical context can cause us to misconnect the dots in ways that lead us to profoundly mistake the Bible's point.

One example of more significant consequences that can result from overlooking historical context emerges from 1 Corinthians 14:33-34. The apostle Paul, one of the most influential leaders in early Christianity, writes to the Christians in the city of Corinth, "Like in all the churches of God's people, the women should be quiet during the meeting. They are not allowed to talk." Read in isolation from any literary or historical context, it certainly appears that the "plain sense" of the statement is a blanket prohibition of women forming any words in church. No preaching, no verbal prayers, no story for the kids. But is this really what Paul had in mind?

To be sure we are understanding Paul as he himself means to be understood, the first thing we must do is back up a bit and explore the larger conversation in which this statement occurs. A little earlier in this same letter, in a discussion about Christian worship Paul says that women who want to pray or prophesy (to prophesy means to deliver an insight from God for the community) should do this with their heads covered (1 Corinthians 11:2-16). This instruction on head-covering might seem somewhat cryptic, but the key thing to notice for now is that Paul clearly expects that women *will* participate in these speech activities during worship and simply provides guidance in how they should attire themselves when speaking.

According to the descriptions we possess of early Christian worship, it appears that believers were encouraged to come to the service with a Scripture or a teaching or an insight from God to share with the community, as God enabled them. Paul encourages this practice. This is apparently exactly the sort of thing in which he expects the women (with their hats on) to participate. But later in the letter, Paul brings up his concern that with so many people showing up with things to say, the gathering could easily dissolve into total chaos. It could turn out rather like the holiday dinner where conversations about the best Marvel film, the price of beans, and the Scrabble prospects of the word *bumfuzzle* are flying across the table all at once, and poor Uncle Joe with his hearing aids is left to puzzle over when Spider-Man, with his fuzzy bum, became such a fan of low-cost soy.

In light of this concern about potential chaos, in 1 Corinthians 14, Paul offers a series of instructions on how to keep the gathering in order: people speaking in tongues (other languages) should talk one at a time and have an interpreter; prophets should take turns delivering messages from God and not try to shout over each other; the women should not talk. But why are these women being singled out as uniquely disruptive in worship? We might be better equipped to answer this question if we have at least a little historical information about the situation of first-century women. Women in this period generally possessed less formal education than men. Unlike men, they also typically did not participate in public lectures where philosophy or other "big ideas" were discussed. It appears that the problem with the women in Corinth is not that they are teaching, leading, or prophesying as they are gifted and called by God. The problem is that, with less background knowledge and less experience in public forums than men, they are prone to *talking during the service*—asking questions, interrupting, murmuring back and forth, and thereby contributing to the general noise and confusion that worries Paul. So along with telling prophets to stop shouting and speak one at a time, Paul tells these women to hush the chatter and save their questions for after the service.[2]

In exploring historical context, maybe the best place to start is simply by approaching the text with a sense of curiosity about the circumstances of the original writers and listeners. You can begin with a very basic question: What was happening in Israel (or Corinth or Rome) at the time that this was written? What would have been their "trending news"? This question explores the general historical situation that the text assumes. Knowing that the prophet Jeremiah is addressing a group of people who were recently forcibly deported to a foreign country gives context to his advice in Jeremiah 29 that they should build houses and make babies. In other words, this isn't lifestyle advice from a restless would-be grandparent; it's a commentary on how long Jeremiah expects that this exile will last (long enough, it seems, for a homebuilding project).

Other basic questions take cultural context into account: What did everyday life look like back then? How might people's picture of family or fishing or financial planning look different from ours today? These questions remind us of the potential gap between our own starting assumptions around these topics and those of people living thousands of years ago and half a world away.

If we come to the text with these sorts of questions in mind, we'll frequently be able to glean important clues about the answers simply by reading carefully. For example, Jeremiah 29:1-2 explicitly, if briefly, describes the situation of the people being addressed. If you're watching for them, you'll be able to pick up on these details and factor them in as you picture the scene. Many, even most, sections of the Bible are relatively self-contained. That is, the text includes enough clues about circumstances that, if we're paying attention, we'll have the information necessary to form a general picture. When, for example, Paul says in Ephesians 4:2, "Conduct yourselves with all humility, gentleness, and patience. Accept each other with love," we don't need to have a precise picture of who has gotten on his last nerve in order to get the point.

However, in other cases our understanding of what's occurring could be significantly aided, even altered, by a bit of historical knowledge we might not personally possess. For this reason, a great way to begin exploring historical context is by acquiring a study Bible. Study Bibles typically provide an overview at the start of each book that offers background about the historical situation the book addresses, setting the scene for the events unfolding. Study Bibles also include brief notes at the bottom of each page that call your attention to additional historical or cultural information potentially relevant to individual verses. These small bits of information, written by people who have dedicated their lives to studying ancient history and culture, can help us envision the context a bit more accurately.[3] If a study Bible whets your appetite to learn even more, biblical commentaries are specialized books that explore in much greater depth specific details about history, language, and culture that illuminate the stories even further.

Whenever you use outside sources like these, keep in mind that because the Bible is an ancient book, much of the historical information we gather is tentative. The evidence for some particular details of background and custom is strong and clearly documented, while in other cases it is less certain. Well-intended students of history may at times put the evidence together differently. This means that any conclusions we draw about the meaning of the text based on information we've drawn from outside it should always be held humbly and tentatively, with openness to new learning.

And while all this historical background is potentially useful, the Bible has been speaking meaningfully for centuries to people who possessed very little additional outside information. At its best, awareness of the role of historical context keeps us from too quickly drawing conclusions based on false assumptions. The pages of the Bible are brought into full life and color when we realize we are reading a story that involves actual people with homes and habits and complications as real and particular as our own.

STORYTIME

Unwrapping Matthew 15:21-39

IT'S A TERRIBLE STORY, really—one that just plain makes Jesus look bad.

A woman approaches Jesus, begging for his help. From the get-go, things are dicey. To begin with, she's female at a time when gender alone renders her insignificant. Second, Matthew labels her a "Canaanite." Canaanite was the term for the people the Israelites killed in Old Testament stories to avoid being tainted by their bad behavior and worship of other gods. In Jesus' time, however, Canaanites did not actually exist as a distinct ethnic group. This makes Matthew's use of the term more akin to a slur, a signal of how a good Jewish person would perceive her: as a religiously suspect foreigner.

This woman has come to Jesus, breaking every barrier, braving known hostility, out of sheer desperation. She is a mother whose young daughter suffers terribly. No one else has been able to help her. And how does Jesus respond to this poor, desperate mother against whom the whole social and religious deck is stacked? Well, first he ignores her, pretends he doesn't even hear her calling after him. Then, after his disciples get tired of her crying and ask him to get rid of her, he replies, "I've been sent only to the people of Israel." And when she finally zigzags past his bodyguards and throws herself on the ground before him, Jesus says, "It's not good to take the children's bread and toss it to dogs."

In three quick hits, Jesus appears to have just confirmed the worst fears of anyone who has ever felt overlooked or unworthy of God's attention: God doesn't notice you. God doesn't want you. God has more important people to worry about.

The Jesus of Matthew 15 seems like, well, a bit of a jerk.

But let's give Jesus the benefit of the doubt for the moment and return to the story a second time to take another look. Only this time, instead of beginning with the woman approaching Jesus in verse 21, let's go back to where the story really starts: Matthew 15:1.

The local religious leaders are, per usual, giving Jesus and company grief. The issue today is that Jesus' followers have been caught eating lunch with unwashed hands. In my world, beyond a few exceptional circumstances—such as a visit to a nursing home during the height of the flu season—practices of handwashing do not tend to rise to the level of moral imperative. But devout first-century Jews had their own theories about the relationship between cleanliness and godliness.

Old Testament Law divided the world into two essential parts. There was what's holy, clean, set apart for God. And there was what's common, unclean, not God's "special stuff." The Jews were a holy people, clean, set apart for a mission from God. The rest of the world generally was not. Eating the wrong food or touching the wrong thing could put a Jew beyond the camp of the holy, out where the rest of the world resided. Over time, among devout Jews a tradition developed in which they washed their hands before eating so as to avoid any chance of being religiously tainted by their interactions with the unwashed masses.

Jesus defends his disciples fiercely in their failure to wash, pointing out that their critics are guilty in their own ways of much more egregious violations of divine law than a simple tradition of hand sanitizing. The disciples are at his back, cheering. "Yeah! You tell 'em, Jesus. Like God really cares about some sticky fingers."

The only trouble is, Jesus keeps on talking. He turns to the crowd and suggests to them that maybe they've been looking at all the wrong things to decide what's in and what's out, who is holy and who is not. What truly makes people clean (or not) is not what they touch, nor what goes into them, but what actually comes out.

The disciples suddenly have a queasy feeling that Jesus is going further than they ever meant to go. After all, it's one thing to get a little dirt on their hands. It's another thing to entirely redefine the categories of what sort of people God is interested in. What Jesus is implying could disrupt the entire system of religious priority by which their own people (the law-abiding people of Israel) always come first and the rest of the world a distant second. They can't be sure that in such a new economy they will come out on top. So they pull Jesus aside and say, "Hey now, Jesus, there's no need to go crazy. You're offending those people over there." (Classic religious code for "You're offending me.")

Jesus is deeply frustrated with his followers. He exclaims, "How could you guys not get this yet, after all this time you've spent with me? Are you really this slow? You're looking at the wrong things to define where God is active and whom God is active with. It's not what goes into a life but what comes out of it that God judges by."

No sooner has Jesus finished speaking these words than a Canaanite woman approaches. Here is a case study in everything they have just discussed. She is totally outside the religious paradigm—female, foreign, tainted. She is everything the disciples have been conditioned to assume God disdains. This is a chance for

them to prove that they finally understand what Jesus is teaching—
that, unlikely as it seems to them, there might be something in this
woman worthy of God's attention. Jesus stays silent and waits to
see how his twelve apprentices will respond. And what do they do?
They ignore her until she makes so much noise they can't take it
anymore. Then they go to Jesus and ask him to get rid of her.

Jesus replies to his disciples, "I've been sent only to the lost
sheep of Israel." Here is the disciples' second test. This sounds like
a clear statement of priority—"You are first; you are my priority,
even at the expense of everybody else." But is it really true? Well,
yes and no. Israel has been chosen by God for a special role in
history, and Jesus does spend most of his time among Jews. But
the question they should be asking is why they were chosen to begin with, why Jesus has focused so much on Israel. God originally
chose to bless this one family so that all peoples could be blessed
through them. Jesus has come to reclaim Israel, to get them back
on track with the mission. If the disciples know their own story,
they understand that the reason God has chosen them is so God
can also choose people like this woman.

Jesus has set his disciples up to push back on the word *only*—
not "only" Israel, but Israel "for the sake of the whole world." But,
as usual, the disciples completely miss their cue. Despairing of
them getting the point, Jesus finally turns his hope toward the
Canaanite woman. He presents her with the same test he presented
his disciples: "It's not good," he says to her, "to take the children's
bread and toss it to dogs."

Here again appears to be a clear statement of priority—"There
are dogs and there are kids; the kids must be fed first." Is this
true? Well, yes and no. In a situation in which children are starving
and there is only one loaf of bread, most people would agree that
a tough decision must be made; you don't feed the dog while the

children waste away. Of course, the crucial question left unanswered is, Who is the dog and who is the kid in this story? Who is God's first choice? Who is the last resort? For the disciples, there is clearly no doubt—they are the kids and she's the canine.

But the woman bypasses this question entirely. She doesn't waste time debating if she is a child or a dog. Instead she just replies, "Even the dogs eat the crumbs that fall off the table." She has no interest in debating abstract order, system, priority, or principle. Because this Canaanite woman understands the crucial truth the disciples have missed: this is not a one-loaf situation. There is enough bread on God's table for everyone—it's piled up and spilling over onto the floor. There's no need to ration, no reason to argue over order or priority, to debate who by birth or action deserves first place. Dogs, kids, sheep, who cares about the label—everyone just come and feast on God's goodness!

Jesus is thrilled by the woman's insight. She is the first one in the story to get it, the first to understand how God's kingdom operates. He turns to his disciples and says, "Do you see this? This is what true faith looks like." Imagine—a Canaanite woman teaching faith to a group of Jewish men.

Viewed in context, this seemingly troubling story completely shifts its shade. Jesus is not blinded to the universal mission of God by his own ethnocentrism and privilege. It is the disciples who are so blinded. Jesus seizes on a timely encounter to set up a critical test. The disciples, predictably, fail, and their blindness is exposed. Offered the same test, the Canaanite woman passes gloriously.

Not only does Jesus confirm the woman's judgment by giving her what she requested, which is healing for her daughter, he does something more: he leaves his encounter with her and goes out to multiply bread (Matthew 15:29-39). "Never mind crumbs under the table," Jesus declares to his disciples. "Give me seven loaves to work with, and I'll give you seven basketfuls to spare." In Jewish tradition, seven was the number of perfection, completion. This, Jesus demonstrates, is the abundance of God's grace: enough for everyone.

Just as the Canaanite woman had spoken.

14

OF DWARVES AND DRAGONS
An Introduction to Genre

Passing through a small southern town, I took a jaunt to the local bookstore. I was initially quite puzzled by the store's classification system. Large, red-lettered signs proclaimed section titles like "Pirates," "Cowboys," "Space," "Royalty," and "Time-Traveling." Under which of these sections, I wondered, could I find a replacement for my dog-eared copy of Tolkien? No sign clearly referenced "Hobbits and/or Dwarves." It was only after several turns down the aisles that the terrifying truth began to dawn. Every section in this store represented a distinct category . . . of paperback romance novel.

In a typical bookstore, books are designated by literary genre: science fiction to the left, biographies to the right, comic books, self-help guides, science texts, poetry, each in their own section. Each genre employs its own "rules for reading" that we largely take for granted. No one reads a sci-fi novel and asks, "Did this really happen?" We understand that the purpose of science fiction is not to tell us facts about the present but to explore possible futures or counterfactual versions of reality. The poet and the scientist both point us toward truth, but each does so with their own accepted modes of presentation. When you open a reference book, you rarely read cover to cover but instead flip straight to the concept you wish to explore.

The Bible is a little bit like a bookstore compressed into one book, bringing together under a single cover a whole variety of literary genres. Each genre follows its own set of writing conventions, and confusion can result if we misidentify which genre we are reading or aren't aware of how that particular genre functions. To expect a future in which a seven-headed dragon literally starts roaming Seattle, looking for people to eat (see Revelation 12), is to deeply misunderstand the way apocalyptic literature is meant to be heard. To read a psalm the same way you read, say, a New Testament letter is likely to be as baffling as reading a dictionary the same way you'd read a graphic novel.

Every genre of literature can contain significant, truthful insights. But the *mode* of truth in which a book speaks also varies according to genre. A proverb, for example, does not speak the same absolute truth as a natural law ("What goes up must come down"). Instead, the mode of truth that is offered by a proverb is a sort of generalized wisdom about how life works out best. When a psalmist cries out in total despair, it is not a definitive statement that there is truly no hope in the cosmos. Rather, such a statement is an emotionally truthful reflection of human experience, of how the world seems to someone who is suffering and who can't feel God's presence anywhere.

While the foundational principles of literary and historical context apply equally to all parts of the Bible, the rules of genre must be learned separately for each set of books.

Interpreting the Bible well requires becoming conversant with the distinctive mechanisms by which each genre delivers its part of the Bible's story. This is our next step, exploring the particular contributions of the Bible's distinct genres and learning to recognize the unique voice in which each speaks its truth.

15

FAREWELL TO CINDERELLA
Old Testament Narrative

Many readers first encountering the Old Testament's lengthy narrative sections assume these stories function rather like an old-school fairy tale. Classic children's literature has a tendency to move in a fairly straight line from darkly messed-up story to moral application. Hansel and Gretel: trust strangers and end up kidnapped and starved and possibly eaten. Cinderella: be good, kind, and selfless and you'll live happily ever after and maybe never have to clean a dirty shower stall again. When we assume the religious significance of the Bible, as I believe we should, our instinct may be to approach the Bible's stories immediately in search of a moral landing place.

The trouble is, the biblical stories are not fundamentally moral tales. In the Bible, sometimes Pinocchio lies and ends up richer for it (see Genesis 26–35). Sometimes Beauty shows up to save a Beast who doesn't really feel like changing and who decides that his life would be easier if he shoved the pesky do-gooder off the nearest turret (see the experiences of most of the prophets). The Bible is full of stories of real human beings making difficult choices in complex situations.

Sometimes their choices are good; sometimes they are bad; sometimes it's hard to tell the difference. And somehow in the midst of all these kinds of choices, God keeps showing up.

The most fundamental rule for interpreting biblical narratives, especially in the Old Testament, is to remember that while every story has a *meaning*, not every story has a *moral*. Every story has a reason for being recorded; not every story lends itself to clear moral judgments or conclusions. Just because something happens in the Bible doesn't mean it should happen, and not every action that seems strange to us is directly condemned.

What we gain from these stories is not a neatly packaged list of dos and don'ts but an expanded imagination for the complexities of life lived together with God. Instead of asking "What's the moral of this story?" and assuming the existence of one definitive answer, it's generally more useful to ask open-ended questions like "Who are these people, and what challenges are they facing? How are they similar to or different from challenges we face today? How are these people encountering God, or what is getting in their way? What might we learn from their failures or successes that could help us navigate the world more fully aligned with God's design?"

Biblical narrative tends to move quickly between action scenes, applying details sparingly. In this way, biblical narrative arguably resembles Stephen King more than Dostoyevsky. Where details cluster and the story's action suddenly slows, it's a bit like when all the cars on the highway abruptly hit their brakes. It's a red flag telling you as the reader to slow down and pay attention—something important is happening nearby that calls for a closer look.

One such section that is short on action but long on detail is 1 Samuel 9:1-10. A young man named Saul is searching for his father's missing donkeys, accompanied by a young servant boy. As the day passes, Saul gets frustrated and impatient and starts to fret over what his father back home must be thinking. He finally throws up his hands and decides to cut his losses. That's when his servant steps in to insist that they keep looking. The servant boy proposes they go ask the local prophet, who reputedly has a direct line with God, to see if God can tell them where the donkeys are. Saul overflows with reasons why this plan will never work—he's not prepared, he's got no money on him, he's got nothing to give the prophet for the favor of his time. That's when the boy pulls a coin from his own pocket and offers to foot the bill himself. They head off to see the prophet, who tells them not to worry because the donkeys have already been found. And then, on the way home, Saul finds twenty dollars. (Not really. Just checking to make sure you're still awake.)

Made for a feature film this scene was not. There's no booby trap, no fight scene, no chariot chase. It has roughly the level of high-stakes action of your average game of peek-a-boo. So in a narrative in which details are applied sparingly, why spend half a page following a guy around as he looks under rocks and says, "Nope, no donkey here"?

If you look at the literary context surrounding this short story, you'll discover this passage serves as the Bible's introduction to Israel's first king. Saul is a head taller than everyone and handsome as a movie star; when he walks into a room, the whole country swoons. What no one in Israel has noticed—and what we will miss too if we don't attend to the red flag waving over the donkey incident—is that Saul is a man with deep, unsettling character flaws. He's riddled with anxieties and worries. He tends to overreact in response to the fears and criticisms of others. He's prone to giving up the moment things get difficult. All it takes is one prepubescent servant boy to lead this so-called leader around by the nose.[1] These characteristics, on display in this first introduction, will continue to play out through Saul's reign, with disastrous effect for everyone. The cluster of seemingly insignificant narrative details turns out to point the reader toward the very heart of the drama. The scene is painting a character portrait that will continue to develop as the story moves along.

What is the moral of the story of Saul and the missing donkeys? It's difficult to derive much of a straightforward moral—except perhaps never to leave home without emergency cash. But remember: biblical narrative is not primarily a collection of morality tales. What we are given in Saul's story is not a rule or behavioral paradigm but a picture of one man's character and its consequences, together with an implied invitation to watch, see, and imagine what we might learn about God and ourselves that could help us navigate our world with greater faithfulness. Engaging the story imaginatively, we might glimpse in Saul a shadow of our own anxieties and the ways they threaten to derail our calling. Or perhaps we might be challenged to reconsider our posture toward prospective leaders, asking where we have been attracted by charm and charisma and prone to overlook critical character flaws.

The beauty and the challenge of reading biblical narratives is that there isn't one right answer to what we make of them. Insight emerges when we find a pivotal intersection between this ancient people's story and our own. Human nature, we will find, has not really changed, and the good news is that neither has God. This means that there is always something to learn from the experiences of those who came before us.

Without question, however, some biblical narratives are harder than others to know what exactly to do with. Second Samuel 13 tells the story of Amnon, son of the famous King David, who rapes his half sister Tamar. David, one of Israel's most celebrated figures, apparently misses the signs of tragedy brewing inside his own household, and after the crime he fails to hold his son meaningfully accountable. The result of this double failure is a chain of further devastation that spreads across David's entire family line.

This tragic tale appears in the Bible without any clear moral lesson spelled out. But at the very least, its inclusion in Scripture acknowledges that horrors occur in even the most "holy" households. This story's appearance honors victims like Tamar by ensuring that their experience is taken seriously as a part of God's own holy story. The purpose of a story like this within the Bible is not to demonstrate what *should* happen but to testify honestly to what *does* happen, even among people of faith, and thereby to open the door for conversations about how we might better respond.

When the presence of a story in the Bible seems especially hard to account for, a good question to ask is what role that particular story is playing within the Bible's entire narrative arc. Remember, all of the hundreds of individual stories in the Bible together contribute to a larger story line recounting God's efforts to reclaim the world. Sometimes the significance of an individual story may be less contained within the story itself than it is related to the story's function in the Bible's larger plotline. A spark plug doesn't do much sitting on its own, but properly attached to the engine, it plays a critical role in helping the whole vehicle move forward. Some stories are much like this: a spark that helps the larger story go where it is headed.

The book of Judges is arguably one such case. Many perplexing and often ugly stories in the book of Judges don't quickly lend themselves to any moral or spiritual landing point, obvious or otherwise. One of the book's final tales describes a man allowing his concubine to be raped in order to protect himself and then, after she dies, cutting her body into pieces and sending out her body parts as a call to war (Judges 19). It's hard to know what to make of such a disturbing story. However, the biggest clue to the story's significance appears in the book's final line: "In those days there was no king in Israel; each person did what they thought to be right" (Judges 21:25). The individual conscience, it appears, is not the most reliable arbiter of moral affairs. The escalating degeneration cataloged by Judges illustrates this point and sets up a need among the people of faith for reliable leadership. The purpose of the story of the brutally mistreated woman may be found primarily in how it moves the biblical plotline forward, explaining why Israel was so desperate for the guidance a kingship could provide.

In every story of the Bible, there are always at least two levels of meaning to consider—the meaning of the story in and of itself, and the role the story plays in the Bible's larger plot. The close-up shot and the wide-angle lens may provide very different perspectives on the story's significance. At times a wide-angle look is especially necessary in order for us to understand what it is we are actually viewing.

16

THE LION BLEATS
Hebrew Poetry

After stories, the second most common literary genre in the Bible is poetry. Around one-third of the Bible is written in some form of poetic line. The most prominent example of biblical poetry is the book of Psalms, the Bible's prayer book, but nearly all the biblical prophets are also written in poetic form, as are several other books, including Job and Song of Songs.

Let's be real—the mere mention of poetry has many people immediately scanning the room for the closest exit. Asked to recite a poem from memory, some of us would be hard-pressed to come up with anything more complex than my personal favorite ditty (discovered printed on a T-shirt):

> Roses are red,
> Bacon is too,
> Poetry is hard,
> Bacon.

Take that, Shakespeare. But ask yourself how many song lyrics you can recite from memory and you'll begin to glimpse why the Bible finds poetry such a useful genre.

To begin with, in very practical terms, poetry is easy to memorize; it has a cadence that lodges itself in your head and sticks there. Poetry is also useful for conveying truths too large for ordinary language. This is why poetry is closely associated with love and romance—it's a medium for capturing feelings too big for everyday speech. The vivid language and imagery of poetry can be emotionally powerful in itself. This fact is especially relevant to anyone interested in human transformation, since modern psychological studies have confirmed what rhetoricians have known since ancient times: people tend to make decisions based on emotions rather than cold, hard logic. If you want to change others' actions, you must move their hearts as much as their heads.

The central ingredient of poetry is metaphor, the bringing together of two seemingly unrelated things in a way that provokes new insights: "Without his morning coffee, Alex was a rabid honey badger, except with less remorse." Psalm 91:13 says that those who trust God "will march on top of lions and vipers." To go to the zoo and climb into the snake tank "because the Bible says so" would be a major genre mistake (and one probably pretty difficult to explain to the zookeeper). The jarring image of someone in sandals walking over a bed of poisonous snakes is intended to provoke an insight about the level of confidence someone can have when they give themselves over to God's care.

To interpret a poetic metaphor, begin by considering what key quality or qualities the two things have in common that the poet is drawing your attention to. In several places in the Bible, God is described as a lion (see Hosea 5:14; 11:10). One of the names Jesus comes to be known by is "the Lion of Judah." There are many qualities of a lion we could imagine a poet attributing to God. A lion is strong and fierce and brave, making it a powerful prospect as a protector. A lion is feared—the mere sound of its roar makes most people weak at the knees. A lion owns the ground it walks on. It dominates its landscape; few enemies can stand against it. Glimpses of God may be seen in all these qualities.

Every metaphor, however, also has a breaking point. Interpreting a metaphor well requires identifying both the shared quality to which it points and also the dissimilarity or limits. In the case of God as lion, the Bible explicitly explores where the metaphor breaks down. In Revelation 5:5, a voice in heaven cries, "Look! The Lion of the tribe of Judah . . . has emerged victorious!" Every head in heaven swivels to give him their attention. But when the curtain is pulled back to reveal the Lion, standing there is a slaughtered Lamb. This is the form that Jesus takes to claim his cosmic victory.

This image of the Lamb in Revelation exposes the limits of the lion metaphor. God is strong, fierce, powerful, victorious, to be feared. But this power is expressed not by devouring enemies but by dying in their place. It's the most shocking metaphor reversal in the Bible, and no one saw it coming precisely because they had bought into the leonine metaphor so completely that they failed to attend to where it might break down. This is always the danger in becoming too cozy with any single metaphor. Serious interpretive errors can result in reading poetry when we fail to recognize where the metaphor comes apart.

English poetry is commonly distinguished from other forms of writing in one of two ways. The first is rhyme, a correspondence of sounds at the end of the lines:

I shall be telling this with a sigh
Somewhere ages and ages hence:
Two roads diverged in a wood, and I—
I took the one less traveled by,
And that has made all the difference.[1]

The other way English poetry is marked is by meter. A good example is Shakespeare's iambic pentameter, where there is a kind of rhythm of the syllables of each line (five repetitions of ba-BOOM):

Shall I compare thee to a summer's day?
Thou art more lovely and more temperate.[2]

The distinguishing characteristics of Hebrew poetry are different from those of English. Hebrew poetry works by creating a balanced rhythm, not primarily of word-sounds but of thoughts or ideas. In the most common poetic form in the Bible, called *synonymous parallelism*, the same idea is repeated twice from a slightly different angle:

A Heaven is declaring God's glory;
B   the sky is proclaiming his handiwork.
A One day gushes the news to the next,
B   and one night informs another what needs to be known.
A Of course, there's no speech, no words—
B   their voices can't be heard—
A   but their sound extends throughout the world;
B   their words reach the ends of the earth.

Notice how each second line (B) in this opening to Psalm 19 echoes the theme of the line that came before it (A).

In other cases, called *antithetic parallels*, the second line (B) forms a contrast with the first (A) instead of an echo. Take Psalm 34:10, for example:

A Even strong young lions go without and get hungry,
B   but those who seek the Lord lack no good thing.

In this verse, the metaphor builds a deliberate contrast with the intended landing point—God's people are *not* like lions in going without food.

In still other cases of biblical poetry, the second line develops the first in some way, taking it further in the same direction (this is called *synthetic parallelism*—see Psalm 23:4). In all forms of parallelism, the interpretive key is to read the lines together, recognizing that they are making not two separate points but a single interrelated one. If in reading a biblical poem you find yourself drawing a conclusion from line A that is too distinct from the point you draw from line B, you might be in danger of overinterpreting the poem, that is, reading something into it that it doesn't mean to say.

With biblical poetry, there is also a real danger of over-reading more generally: dissecting the piece so far that it begins to look less like art and more like the remains of a dissected sophomore biology frog. Even as we attend to individual words, phrases, and metaphors, it's also important to step back and simply experience the poem and the emotions it evokes. That experience is crucial to understanding not just what the poem says but where it means to move us.

The Bible's premier poetic book, the Psalms, contains many categories of psalms and prayers. Some offer praise to God for God's divine attributes. Others thank God for God's particular activities in human history. Some psalms focus on Israel's kings, others on the city of Zion (another name for ancient Israel's capital, Jerusalem). The most common form of psalm in the Bible is the lament, a poem expressing individual or corporate suffering.

Probably the most troubling kind of psalm in the Bible, and the hardest for most readers to know what to do with, is the imprecatory (or cursing) psalm. Psalm 137:9, for example, directs the following curse toward Babylon, the national enemy of Israel:

> A blessing on the one who seizes your children
> and smashes them against the rock!

The psalms—at their best, and at their worst—present an honest expression of human feeling and the whole range of human experience. However, the presence of such honest expression in the pages of the Bible does not automatically entail an endorsement of the feelings themselves. With their raw and open range of emotions, the psalms remind us that biblical religion isn't just about abstract ideas of God; it's about an invitation to an intimate relationship into which we can bring the truth of ourselves and our lives.

Cursing psalms like Psalm 137 serve several important functions within that relationship. First, they offer a model for transparency. They tell us we don't have to sugarcoat; God can take our honesty. We can bring our real emotions, however ragged or ugly, openly and without fear into the presence of God. They'll even loan us words to express emotions that might otherwise stay bottlenecked within, slowly poisoning us.[3]

Second, cursing psalms acknowledge that evil is real and worth naming as such. To be clear, naming evil and our feelings about it does not give us the right to take the response into our own hands. Quite the contrary; the psalms name evil and then call for God to intervene. The expectation of God's active response keeps us free from pursuit of revenge.

Third, there are occasions when speaking our misshapen feelings aloud, giving concrete form to our hidden hatred, self-righteousness, and resentment, can actually be the first step toward necessary inward change. The imprecatory psalms drag the monster out of the dark closet and force it to expose itself, to stand there with all its warts and scales in the full daylight.

Nothing that is carried into the light of God remains unaltered by it. Sometimes the only way to slay the beast lurking inside us is to tell the truth about it and to present it to God.

17

HOLY HAIRCUTS
The Law

I t is not for nothing that the literary genre most commonly associated with the Bible is the law code. The Old Testament contains no fewer than 613 laws, addressing everything from sex to mold infestations to whether burgers should be served with cheese or bacon (answer: guacamole). Modern readers often find themselves repelled by these laws, which seem alternately obscure, outdated, and burdensomely intrusive on personal liberty. But surprisingly, this was not ancient Israel's feeling about their law book. The longest chapter of the Bible, Psalm 119, spends all 176 verses celebrating the Law as one of God's premier gifts to the Israelite community.

We might conclude from this that some people just have quite strange tastes—after all, rumor has it at least a few Crocs shoe owners actually bought them on purpose. But in truth, Israel had very good reasons for their appreciation.[1] Many people think of law as that which restricts us from doing things we'd otherwise desire—say, driving ninety miles an hour down the highway or walking the rottweiler without being forced to carry home five bags of steaming poop. But the point of the Law given to Israel was not to spoil people's fun. Rather, if God is the world's architect, it stands to reason that God is in the best position to understand how it operates. Living against the basic structure of God's design is like swimming against the current or walking up the down escalator: it can be done, but it sure makes everything harder. The Law offered Israel insight on how to live well in the world, in line with the underlying shape of God-ordered reality.

When a mother tells her child, "Don't play with fire," she is not making up an arbitrary rule to reinforce her own sense of power; she's teaching her kid how to live within the laws of the universe without damaging himself or others. This is not so different from what God does in giving Israel a law that prohibits adultery. Much like rules for behaving around open flames, the law against adultery provides instruction on how to handle a hot, powerful force (in this case, sex) so that it serves joy and life instead of threatening them.

It is no coincidence that the Law was first given to the people of Israel as they were coming out of slavery. God's intent was not to steal back the freedom God had just won for them but to *guard* that freedom, making sure new kinds of chains didn't catch them unaware. When the Law says "Do not covet," the purpose isn't to stop anyone from possessing something good but rather to prevent the goodness of life from being consumed by empty longing. When the Law says "Don't make idols," the point isn't to ban good art but rather to keep imaginations from getting trapped in some projection of God that is less than the whole. It's a bit as if the Law is saying, with respect to different areas of life, "Don't nibble that particular chicken if you don't want a bad case of food poisoning."

Beneath many laws that seem obscure or distant from the modern world lie pivotal insights into God's character and passions. Leviticus 23:22 instructs the Israelites not to harvest the edges of their fields. At first glance, this law appears to have little to say to someone like me, who lives in a city apartment and who has repeatedly proven herself unable to keep even a potted cactus alive. But if we look closer at this command, asking what it reveals about God, we might notice that the stated reason for leaving the edges of a field untouched is so the poor and the foreigner can harvest there and make a living. These vulnerable populations appear to be of special concern to God.

But some Old Testament laws don't seem to fit the purposes just described, providing wisdom for living or insight into the interests of God. Leviticus 19:19 declares, "Do not wear clothes made from two kinds of material"—a command seemingly oblivious to the considerable merits of wrinkle-free polyester-cotton. Other complex sets of laws cover what is permissible for Israelites to eat or to touch or to plant, and even how men are allowed to cut their hair. Many laws reflect ancient logic, foreign to us today, which assumed there were things people could do (like develop a particular kind of rash) or touch (like a dead body) that would make them ritually "unclean" and therefore unfit for God's presence. As we will explore in a later chapter, Jesus openly challenged this logic in his ministry, touching the untouchable and suggesting that it's what comes out of mouths, not what goes into them, that makes people unclean.

But in contemplating what function these puzzling laws might have served in their original setting, it's worth recalling why Israel was chosen by God to start with. The family of

Israel was called to be *holy*, a term that means "set apart." They were meant to be set apart from the destructive, self-seeking ways the rest of the world had adopted so that Israel could model an alternative, more beautiful way of living under the rule of God.

The Israelites were rescued from Egypt and brought to a new land with this mission in mind. However, the mission entrusted to Israel was precarious. Virtually all immigrant communities eventually discover how difficult it is to preserve a distinctive culture and set of values. A second generation, born in a land where Tinder and twerking pass as "normal," quickly picks up the practices they see every day around them.

Israel was in constant danger of losing sight of their mission, adopting their neighbors' broken patterns, starting to blend in. Therefore, Israel's law code includes provision for small, daily, visible reminders that belonging to God always entails a different kind of normal. Every time the Israelites dress in the morning or eat a meal, they are reminded, "God lives right here among us, and we've been set apart to model God's alternative vision for the world. Every single thing we do is in relationship with God, and that means that it's all going to look a bit beautifully strange." If Israel had a national motto, it would be "Odd for God."

One specific category of laws that appear prominently in the Old Testament are those involving the sacrificial system. On various occasions, the Israelites are instructed to bring a sacrifice or offering to the temple, the designated place of worship. In some cases, an animal was sacrificed on the altar to serve as a kind of "ransom" or stand-in for the life of the petitioner who'd sinned against God and provoked God's anger.

A priest would burn the sacrifice as an offering to God and on God's behalf declare forgiveness to the petitioner. Other times sacrifices might be offered in celebration of the harvest, in gratitude for some special blessing, or in fulfillment of a vow. In these cases, a portion of meat or grain would be burned as a gift to God, and the rest of the food would be eaten by the priests and also frequently by the worshipers who'd brought the offering. It was a little like gathering friends and family for a barbecue dinner, with God as the honored guest at the head of the feasting table.

Reading the wide range of Old Testament laws, it's tempting to assume they should be divided into two broad categories: those that are culturally relative (no poly-cotton) and those that are universally binding (no murdering). In practice, however, it's surprisingly difficult to find objective standards to define how we know which is which, other than "Murder is obviously bad," "Cheeseburgers are delicious," and "No one I know has leprosy." That's because this distinction is foreign to the Law itself. The Law served Israel both as a document governing faith and as a kind of national constitution. Religious and civil elements, even public health policies, all show up in the Law intertwined.

The Law in its entirety was given to Israel as part of a covenant—a formal agreement established between God and Israel right after they left Egypt. According to the terms of this agreement, Israel would receive God's blessing and protection if they obeyed all the Law's stipulations. If they did not, God would withdraw God's favor and things would fall apart faster than a pair of three-dollar flip-flops. The writers of the New Testament would later explain that Israel's ancient law code is no longer binding in any part on followers of

Jesus, because followers of Jesus live under a new covenant. The conditions of this new covenant are met not by us keeping Israel's Law but by Jesus' own complete obedience to God and his sacrifice on our behalf. God's blessing, God's favor, is offered to any who tie themselves to Jesus.

In the view of the New Testament, the Law was a little like training wheels. It was useful for practicing how to navigate in responsiveness to God. It helped Israel keep their balance, avoid falling off the road into thorny ditches, until Jesus arrived. (Or at least that was the intent.) But now the training wheels are off. When people live in submission to Jesus and respond to the turn-by-turn guidance of his Spirit, the true purpose of the Law is fulfilled.

The Old Testament Law is not binding today on Christians, who live under the new covenant of Jesus. But that doesn't make it irrelevant. We can still glean insights from Israel's Law that shape imagination for what it might look like to be people set apart for God, even in a very different time. For example, Exodus 23:4-5 instructs the Israelites, "When you happen to come upon your enemy's ox or donkey that has wandered off, you should bring it back to them. When you see a donkey that belongs to someone who hates you and it's lying down under its load and you are inclined not to help set it free, you must help set it free."

Now, it's true that this is ancient Israel's law, not ours. It is also a fact that—at least as of the time of this writing—I've personally never had occasion to run across a wandering ox or toppled donkey. But this law, at its heart, is not about oxen but about people you dislike. Beyond its limited viability as a time-specific law, this law might spark insight into how those who belong to God relate to their enemies: "When you happen to come upon your nemesis's car on the side of the road with its tire blown, instead of throwing a wad of gum at the back of your enemy's head as you zip by, perhaps you should stop and help her change the tire, whether you feel like it or not."

Now *that's* an imagination shaped like God's.

18

THE OUTSIDERS
The Prophets

You might describe the biblical prophet as the ultimate outsider. The prophets operated in the period during and immediately after the monarchies of Israel and Judah. The king, love him or hate him, was your classic politician. He listened to his advisors (sometimes) and kept the institution running. He made decisions about taxes and national security. If he was a good king, he concerned himself with defending ordinary people's interests; if he was a bad king, he spent more time expanding his palace, hobnobbing with elites, and tippling drinks with pretentious names like Blue Electric Pineapple Harem.

The prophets, by contrast, operated outside the formal power structure of the institution. Rather than attend to the voices of the national interest groups or bend to the pressure of Big (Olive) Oil, their job was to attend solely to the interests of God.[1] The prophets spoke to the general populace but especially to the nation's leaders, delivering messages from God about current affairs.

The nations of Israel and Judah were in a covenant relationship with God. An ancient covenant worked rather like a modern contact. The people had agreed to follow God and live in line with God's desires as expressed in the Law. In exchange, God promised to bless them—with produce, kids, and cows—or to punish them—with famine, war, plague, drought, cattle disease, destruction, exile, and death—as their behavior warranted. (That Deuteronomy 28 takes roughly four times as long to describe the punishments as it does the rewards suggests something about God's level of optimism regarding the outcome of this arrangement.)

The prophets tended to this covenant at the foundation of their nation's life. They were the nation's spiritual IRS, keeping the people accountable for their choices, letting them know how they were doing in keeping with the Law and what God was doing in response. Needless to say, the prophets were rarely the most popular guests on the dinner party circuit.

Many people hear the word *prophecy* today and imagine it involves something like fortune-telling—"The night of the next full moon, a young boy digging in a field will stumble on the Tesseract, a weapon that will change the tide of every future battle." However, the primary job of the biblical prophet was not to read the stars (or cards, or tea leaves, or entrails, or whatever was popular back then) in hopes of gleaning random insider information about what's around the bend of time. Rather, the prophets of Israel and Judah are keenly attuned to the link between choice and consequences. While they do frequently discuss the future, especially the *near* future, their central focus is not on making predictions "from nowhere" but on explaining to their people in concrete terms where their own current actions are leading them.

In the prophets' worldview, the future is not set in stone in a way that can be unambiguously "foretold." Because God is fundamentally responsive and relational, alternative futures are always open. A prophet can announce that the people's choices have set them up for a looming disaster. But that disaster might not strike if the people heed the message and change course. The prophets generally lay out the options and their consequences: choose God's way, and your sheep will breed like rabbits; persist in rebellion, and don't be surprised when you end up eating placenta for lunch (see Deuteronomy 28:55-57 for that little gem).

Israel begins its monarchy as one unified nation, but conflicts over leadership quickly splits the nation in two, with Israel situated to the north and Judah to the south. Each nation has its own succession of kings and follows its own spiritual and moral trajectory. Consequently, each nation also has its own set of prophets who arise to address its unique circumstances. Jonah, Amos, and Hosea are prophets of the north, while Obadiah, Joel, Micah, Isaiah, Zephaniah, Nahum, Habakkuk, and Jeremiah are prophets of the Southern Kingdom.

The prophets are especially busy in the later years of both monarchies. This is not surprising, given that prophets serve as a kind of early warning system for imminent disaster. The frequency and severity of prophetic messaging is like a board game timer beeping faster and faster, warning that the window for game-changing action is quickly closing.

One thing to watch for with the prophets is their specific accusations of the ways the people of faith have departed from the good desires of God. A few central concerns occupy a great deal of prophetic real estate. One significant concern revolves around idolatry. Prophetic texts reference prostitution with a frequency that might make you wonder how Israelites even find time to eat between all this sleeping around. But in many cases, the biblical prophets are drawing on prostitution as a metaphor for how Israel and Judah are cheating on God. The whole country, the prophets claim, has turned into one giant spiritual red-light district. The people are giving themselves, body and soul, not to the God who loves them passionately but to forces with nothing to offer them but a few empty minutes behind a tree.

Another major theme of the prophets is God's concerns about treatment of the poor, widows, orphans, and foreigners. The prophets suggest that a very good status check of Israel's covenantal health would simply be to take the pulse of their overall care for the vulnerable. As people are with their community's neediest members, so they are with God.

In many circles today, the term *prophet* has become synonymous with political advocacy for social justice. Social justice is indeed a matter that evokes a great deal of passion from the biblical prophets. But in interpreting the Bible's prophetic books, it's crucial to recognize that concerns about social justice and idolatry travel together intertwined. The primary job of the prophet was to mediate the covenant between Israel and God. Most prophetic messages were directed not to a "secular" nation but to a religious community explicitly bound by a common commitment to faith. In this sense, the "Israel" the biblical prophets address has much more in common with the church than a modern nation-state. The prophet's message was a call back to the accountable relationship with God from which all true justice springs.

"What the Lord requires from you," Micah memorably declares, is "to do justice, embrace faithful love, and walk humbly with your God" (Micah 6:8). In the prophetic imagination, proper worship and social ethics are not two concerns but one. Right relationships between people and loyal devotion to God cannot be separated. The former without the latter is a skeleton without a beating heart. The latter without the former is a bleeding heart without hands or feet. There is no justice without true faith; there is no true faith without justice.

For many readers, one special challenge in encountering the prophets is their use of some especially violent or disturbing metaphors. Hosea, for example, describes Israel as a cheating wife whom God threatens to "strip naked" and "slay with thirst" (Hosea 2:3 NIV). It's certainly valid to ask questions about how such metaphors might shape those who read them today, and there's no simple answer for what to do with the unsettling imagery. But as we wrestle with the particularities of biblical rhetoric, there are at least a few considerations worth keeping in mind.

First, in communication, audience matters. The original audience of Hosea likely was almost entirely men, reared in a patriarchal culture, who were utterly certain of the absolute loyalty owed them by their wives but who had no sense at all of any loyalty they themselves owed God. Hosea's metaphor flips their own paradigm on them, forcing them to stand temporarily in the shoes they'd created for women. The shock of this dislocation is meant to jerk them awake to the shocking nature of their own behavior.

Second, keep in mind that the biblical writers' own voices are an integral part of the shape of Scripture. The prophets listen for the message God is speaking to the people (such as "God demands your absolute loyalty"). Like all biblical writers, however, they also process and communicate that message using language and metaphors relevant to their experience. For better or worse, this is how God's words always move—filled with divine breath, but also wearing human skin.

You might notice that considerably fewer books in the Bible speak to the Northern Kingdom than to their sister kingdom in the south. There's one simple reason for this: the Northern Kingdom doesn't last long. The behavior of Israel in the north devolved more quickly than Judah's in the south, and consequently, Israel's kingdom is destroyed in 722 BCE by the empire of Assyria. The southern kingdom of Judah holds on for almost 150 more years. If the prophets' tone during this period gets a bit testy, well, it's because they're watching Judah barrel toward the same cliff's edge that Israel just fell over. People are ignoring every call to slow down and heed their path. In 586 BCE, after remaining determinedly deaf to centuries of prophetic warnings, the Southern Kingdom finally falls as well, conquered by the empire of Babylon.

After the destruction of Judah, some of the prophets, like Jeremiah, Isaiah, Ezekiel, and Daniel, continue to speak to remnants of Judah who are now scattered in exile. In keeping with the contrarian nature of the prophetic job, here the tone shifts considerably. Where before the prophecies were all dire warnings, now that everyone has despaired, the prophetic message turns to hope: God is a God of second (and seventieth) chances. Even if all that's left of their dreams is a giant urn of ashes, God may yet perform an impossible resurrection (see Ezekiel 37). Prophets like Haggai, Zechariah, and Malachi continue to work after the exile finally ends and the people return to their shattered land and begin to rebuild. These prophets encourage the people to make sure this God-given sequel doesn't just turn into a bad remake of the same old movie.

While the covenant the prophets enforce is not binding today, as with the Law itself there is much we can learn from the prophetic books about God's character and desires. The prophets remind us that people tend to become much like whatever they worship—what they honor with their attention, their resources, their love and loyalty. They point out the indissoluble link between care for the vulnerable and relationship with God. They help us recognize God's judgment as an extension of God's mercy. For the prophets, God's judgment is an expression of God's unbreakable commitment to rectify wrongs, put an end to oppression, and deliver us from the addiction to violence, greed, and self-reliance by which we damage our neighbors and do harm to our own souls.

19

HOW TO SAVE YOUR MARRIAGE
Wisdom Literature

There is a vastly underrated difference between wisdom and knowledge. Knowledge involves comprehending the combustion mechanism by which a car can go from zero to sixty in under ten seconds. Wisdom involves the decision about whether to test this capacity on the street in front of the local cop's house.

Wisdom means understanding the world in such a way that you are able to live well within it. It has an action orientation, and it possesses a sharp eye both for patterns and for the unique exigencies of each particular situation.

The "wisdom literature" of the Bible includes an eclectic set of books that primarily have in common their keen interest in practical questions of life. Perhaps the best-known wisdom book in the Bible is Proverbs, a book packed with pithy advice. Want to know a single sentence that just might save your marriage? Proverbs has got you covered: "Greeting a neighbor with a loud voice early in the morning will be viewed as a curse" (Proverbs 27:14). You're welcome.

Most proverbs are fairly simple to understand. The difficulty tends to arise in practice, when a proverb flatly asserts something that seems directly contradicted by experience. Proverbs 28:20 reads, "Reliable people will have abundant blessings, but those with get-rich-quick schemes won't go unpunished." Most of us would be pleased if this were always true, but the Nigerian prince requesting your bank account number might beg to differ. Or take Proverbs 29:17—"Instruct your children; they will give you peace of mind and bring delight into your life." Plenty of parents tearing out their hair wonder where exactly their story went so wrong.

Here's the thing: a proverb is neither a promise nor a guarantee of any particular outcome. It does not operate with the inexorability of gravity. A proverb is a generalization, a mode of truth always grounded in the phrase "all things being equal . . ." A proverb offers good advice on how generally to live in line with the shape of God's world. But a generalized truth is exactly the sort that lends itself to a myriad of contextual exceptions.

In interpreting the proverbs, it's useful to watch for ways that various proverbs expose each other's limits. Proverbs 26:4 instructs, "Don't answer fools according to their folly, or you will become like them yourself." (As we might say today, "Don't stoop to their level!") But the very next verse, Proverbs 26:5, tells another side to the story: "Answer fools according to their folly, or they will deem themselves wise." There are times, perhaps, when puncturing an overinflated head might just save a life. The question isn't which proverb is right and which is wrong. These two generalized truths exist in tension with each other. Both must be considered in order to wisely discern which may apply to the case in point.

The central word of Ecclesiastes is *hevel*, which literally means "vapor." "Everything is vapor!" the author cries at the start (Ecclesiastes 1:2; CEB translates this as "pointless"). This book explores how human beings should live in light of the fleeting and often arbitrary nature of life, in which nothing in the world seems to truly progress and where the jar seemingly gets passed on to somebody else the moment you've finished the hard work of loosening the lid.

The writer of Ecclesiastes, who styles himself "the Teacher," offers pragmatic advice: in the face of all this pointlessness, you'd best get on with eating and drinking and "enjoying your wife" (wink, wink). But then all of a sudden at the end, the book takes an unexpected twist: "So this is the end of the matter; all has been heard. Worship God and keep God's commandments because this is what everyone must do. God will definitely bring every deed to judgment, including every hidden thing, whether good or bad" (Ecclesiastes 12:13-14).

One way to interpret the seemingly contradictory counsel of Ecclesiastes is to suggest that most of the book represents false wisdom in need of correction. All this talk of "vapor" and "meaninglessness" and tossing it all to the wind simply sets up the final landing: "Psych! Actually, everything I just said is wrong; life really does have meaning, because God's actually going to judge what use you make of it. Gee, I hope everyone finished the whole book and made it to this part."

If we read this book on a second level, in light of the Bible's larger story, it might also be possible to understand it as an expression of existential despair that can only truly be answered when Jesus comes on the scene. What both of these readings have in common is that the discussion in Ecclesiastes about the futility of life is understood to build toward recognition of the opposite—because God is involved, there is meaning in everything.

But while there is much to be said for seeing Ecclesiastes's longing for meaning as ultimately answered in Jesus, there's also value in reading the book in a more straightforward fashion and assuming the author simply means exactly what he says. For workaholics who sleep with cell phones in hand and whose seatbelts are stained with the remnants of a thousand drive-through meals, Ecclesiastes offers a helpful reality check: "Bad news, buckaroo. You're not as important as you think. That thing you're spending your life building? It's already turning to dust. Even if you do something truly great, like curing cancer or ridding the planet of selfie sticks, in a few decades nobody but a handful of trivia nerds will even remember your name." In this reading, the divine wisdom of Ecclesiastes might be its call to more fully inhabit the present—to cherish relationships, savor small gifts, show up to the whole of our precious, fleeting human lives.

Both Christians and Jews have struggled to know what to do with the steamy poetry of Song of Songs.[1] Many have sought to resolve the mystery of the presence of this book in the Bible by interpreting it as an allegory for the spiritual intimacy shared between God and God's people. Now before you start rolling your eyes, it should be noted that several other books of the Bible, including Hosea, do employ romantic metaphors to talk about relationship with God. There's just one significant problem in seeing this as the primary meaning of this particular book: the name of God is not mentioned a single time.

Probably the best way to interpret this unusual book of wisdom is as exactly what it appears to be: a celebration of romance and sex as a good part of God's design. While religion has an unfortunate habit of dressing talk about sex in a thick shroud of shame and burying it deep inside an impregnable fortress of spike-topped "thou shalt nots," Song of Songs suggests an alternative place to start the conversation. It begins with God's original creation refrain: "Heck yes! This is such a good idea!" It begins with a vivid portrait of the divine gift of sex and of its beauty set within the landscape of a fully God-ordered life.[2]

The book of Job is counted by many as among the most challenging texts in the Bible. Most of the book consists of an extended dialogue between a man named Job and four close friends about the cause of human suffering. Job, who has recently suffered unthinkable tragedies, occasionally breaks from the dialogue with his friends to throw back his head and hurl full-throated protests at God.

If you pull a section from the book of Job at random, you'll find within it a variety of responses offered to Job in his agony: God is just, and therefore one way or another, people must get what they deserve; those who live with integrity will be rescued and blessed, and the unrighteous will suffer disaster; just repent, and God will restore you. These explanations, offered by Job's friends, closely echo other parts of the Bible. Specifically, this is how the Old Testament Law said the covenant with God worked: if people obeyed, good things would happen; if they didn't, disaster would strike. The friends' responses to Job's situation are deeply biblical.

There's just one problem: they're also wrong.

This is the dilemma at the heart of the book of Job: none of the well-established Old Testament truths apply in Job's case. He has been perfectly faithful to God and suffered anyway. It's as if we've suddenly arrived at the edge of the biblical horizon, the point of singularity where all the known truths simply fall apart.

The book of Job challenges reductionist answers to the problem of suffering. It exposes limits to any conclusion, easy to draw from other parts of the Bible (especially the Law and the proverbs), that obedience and blessing, suffering and sin, are inevitably linked. The book of Job never offers a clear answer for why the innocent suffer, but it does put an important check on excessive religious certainty. It confronts us with the limits of what we can know and reminds us that the vastness of God's wisdom reaches far beyond our grasping.

The example of Job himself both offers permission to wrestle honestly with God and provokes the humbling recognition that as finite human beings, we will never be in a position to take in the whole of what God sees. In a world full of such mysteries, perhaps the most useful lesson of all is the one we can glean from Job's friends: faced with another person's suffering, often the better part of wisdom is to sit down, shut up, and just share in the weeping.

20

SHOOTING SNAKES
The Gospels

Imagine five documentary filmmakers descending on Florida to chronicle the exploits of local python hunters. Even if they each go to the same small towns and talk to the same people, the result would still likely be five very different films. This isn't because one is telling the truth and the others are lying. Rather, five independent people with their own backgrounds and questions will invariably experience events differently. They'll focus their cameras on different details, cut some scenes and highlight others according to the story line they find compelling. And which thread of the story they choose to follow might also be affected by their intended audience—say, the community of concerned environmentalists versus the fan base of the cult classic film *Snakes on a Plane*.

Our job as interpreters would probably be easier if the first followers of Jesus had gotten together and composed one definitive version of "Jesus: The Authorized Biography" without any repetitions, redundancies, or apparent contradictions. But to their credit, the early Christians recognized that a sequence of events as complex and world changing as the life, death, and resurrection of Jesus Christ was worth exploring from a variety of angles. Therefore, instead of consolidating all the stories circulating about Jesus into one master narrative, the church preserved four accounts, called gospels, each with its own unique perspective on Jesus and his work.

Each gospel writer shapes his telling with a different audience in mind, pulling on threads of the story he finds most important and weaving them together into a signature design. Each one makes his own decisions about what scenes to include and how to order them, what details to highlight, and what wording to use to make the meaning clear. The intent of these writers is not simply to record history but to *interpret* history for their communities, to help their own specific audiences understand the significance of all Jesus said and did.

When the same story appears in multiple gospels and comes out differently, it's often because the writers are highlighting different aspects of the event's significance that are relevant to their diverse communities. Matthew portrays Jesus as teaching "Blessed are the poor in spirit" (Matthew 5:3 NIV), while Luke depicts Jesus as saying starkly "Blessed are you who are poor" (Luke 6:20 NIV). To ask "Which author quoted Jesus correctly?" misses the point. Both authors offer truthful applications of Jesus' teachings to communities in different circumstances, much like a preacher today might give a different sermon to residents of a nursing home than to a room of middle school campers. One gift of having multiple gospel accounts is the insight we gain into how Jesus' teachings were applied by his followers in varied real-world contexts.

The first three books in the New Testament, Matthew, Mark, and Luke, are often called the synoptic ("to see together") gospels because of substantial overlap in the stories they tell. Only 3 percent of the gospel of Mark is unique to Mark. In some cases, Mark's stories are repeated in Matthew or Luke almost word for word, leading scholars to suspect that Matthew and Luke used Mark as a source. (When your Lord and Master rises from the dead, no one has time to fret over the nuances of plagiarism.) On many other occasions, the same story appears in two or more gospels with slightly different details or timing. Where these differences occur, it's useful to note them and ask how each author's unique telling might shift the emphasis or cause us to see the event's significance in a different light.

The gospel of John was likely the last gospel written, and roughly 90 percent of the material is unique to John. This could be because John simply did not have access to Matthew, Mark, or Luke. It's also possible, however, that John had read these accounts and was deliberately working to supplement stories already told, offering his own take on what should be emphasized about Jesus. John knew the church was approaching a new stage, in which the firsthand witnesses to Jesus' life and death would no longer be around. Recognition of the questions this new situation would bring could explain John's interest in Jesus' teachings about God's ongoing presence in the Spirit.

You'll probably notice as you read through the Gospels that each one has its own distinctive flavor. Mark's gospel, likely the earliest, appears to have been written in a hurry. Mark has no patience for baby talk; he jumps straight to the meat of Jesus' ministry. His gospel plays a lot like an action movie, full of drama and movement. It drives relentlessly toward the cross, with nearly half the book devoted to Jesus' final journey to his death. Mark's portrait of Jesus highlights his identity as the Son of God.[1] With respect to everyone else in the story, Mark maintains a rather dark tone, emphasizing both the fierce opposition of religious authorities to Jesus and the consistent failures of his own, often clueless disciples.

Matthew's gospel is situated as a bridge between the Old and New Testaments. For Matthew, Jesus is the promised Messiah and the culmination of Israel's entire history. His favorite phrases—"it was written" and "this was to fulfill what was said"—identify links and echoes between Jesus' story and earlier parts of the Bible. Matthew weaves the teachings of Jesus together into longer, composite sermons. Like Moses, the Old Testament figure who met with God on a mountain to receive Israel's Law, Jesus climbs a mountain and delivers his own radical interpretation of the Law in the famous section of Matthew's gospel commonly known as the Sermon on the Mount (Matthew 5–7). All these features, taken together, make it likely that Matthew was writing with a Jewish community in mind.

By contrast, the gospel of Luke was probably written for a Roman audience. Like Matthew, Luke starts his story with Jesus' family tree, but instead of topping the tree with Abraham, father of the Jewish people, as Matthew does, Luke stretches all the way back to Adam, father of humanity. Many of his stories also feature Gentiles (non-Jews) and women as central characters. Luke exhibits special concern for the poor and a keen interest in Jesus' teachings on money. His gospel is especially full of healing stories and parables.

Luke is particularly unique as the only gospel writer to compose a sequel. The book of Acts carries on with key threads of Luke's plot, demonstrating how the teachings and story of Jesus played out in the lives of his followers after he was gone. Given this "part 2," it's probably no surprise that Luke also focuses on the Holy Spirit and is the only gospel writer to mention the church by name.

John stands out among the gospels not only because of its unique combination of stories but also because of its distinctive perspective on Jesus himself. John is a theologian, and when he writes about Jesus, it's important to him to clearly indicate not just what happened but what it really meant. John's gospel focuses on Jesus' ministry in the region of Jerusalem, rather unlike the other gospels, whose stories often come from Jesus' ministry farther north. While Luke's portrait of Jesus highlights his humanity, in John it is Jesus' divinity that shines. While Matthew arranges Jesus' teachings in composite sermons, John often presents Jesus' teachings in the form of extended dialogues. John's gospel also has a distinctively dualistic (black-and-white) bent to it—either you are with Jesus fully or you are against him—which might reflect the fact that he was writing at a time in which the church faced increased opposition, even persecution.

Literary context is especially important in interpreting the Gospels, because the gospel writers are quite strategic in how they arrange their material. Their books frequently progress in a kind of stair-step motion in which each story connects to and builds on the one that came before. Reading each short story or unit of teaching in light of what comes right before it and right after it often calls attention to key aspects of its meaning.

Matthew 18:15-20 explores the practice of discipline in the Christian community, suggesting that an unrepentant church member should be treated like "a Gentile and tax collector." Some in history have interpreted this passage as a mandate to give an offender the communal silent treatment, cutting off all social contact. However, the story immediately preceding this passage is a parable describing God's determined pursuit of a lost sheep that has wandered from the safety of the flock. Jesus' teaching on church discipline is put in the context of a God who'll travel to earth's end to avoid losing a single person. Matthew has deliberately arranged his material so that side-by-side stories inform and interpret each other.

Many of Jesus' most memorable teachings, like the teaching about the lost sheep, come in the form of parables, short stories featuring scenes and images from ordinary life. Parables work by lowering your defenses, by getting under your guard. In this way, they function much like jokes. Take, for example, the joke someone told me recently:

"Knock, knock."
"Who's there?"
"Control freak. Now you say, 'Control freak who?'"

This joke works precisely by disrupting our cultural expectation of how a knock-knock joke ends. In a similar fashion, parables use familiar images to create expectation; you think you know where the story is going. But somewhere along the way, expectations are subverted. The story takes a twist. The landing point turns out to be different from what you supposed; the truth catches you off balance.

The key to interpreting a parable is to place yourself in the shoes of the original listeners and ask what the parable has set you up to expect. Then look for the way the parable turns or subverts those expectations. Keep in mind that this might require imaginatively closing the historical distance, since the expectations of people living thousands of years ago might be different from those that occur to you today.

When the gospel writers want to sum up Jesus' entire ministry, they frequently say things like this: Jesus "announced the good news of the kingdom and healed every disease and sickness among the people" (Matthew 4:23). This "kingdom," the primary topic of Jesus' parables and teachings, is shorthand for a world at peace, finally fully aligned with God's more beautiful design. Through his ministry, Jesus announces to people that this kingdom is close, that the new world is coming soon. The healings and miracles he performs are not incidental to his message but a demonstration of it. They're the appetizer course, the first tastes of the new world, of what reality will be when all creation is finally brought into full submission to the rule of Christ. Not everything is yet as it should be, but wherever people begin to gather in shared allegiance to Jesus, the first sprouts of the new world start to spring up and grow.

STORYTIME

Unwrapping Luke 16:1-13

THERE ONCE WAS a very rich man who owned a national chain of car dealerships. Since he spent most of his time at corporate headquarters in New York City, he decided to hire managers to look after the day-to-day operations of his West Coast locations.

But after some time had passed, the owner began to get calls about the manager of his Los Angeles dealership. It seemed that the LA manager had been adding fake surcharges to the purchase price in order to take advantage of customers who didn't read the fine print, and then pocketed the proceeds. He'd been spotted joyriding new convertibles down the coastal highway and using the company card to throw lavish beachside parties—even writing off Oakleys as a "business expense." Finally the owner sent an email to his renegade manager consisting of just two sentences: "I'm flying in Friday. Get the spreadsheets in order."

When the manager received this email on his iPhone 1002 as he was flying down the highway, he nearly wrecked the car. "What am I going to do?!" he thought. "I'm about to be fired. The only people hiring these days are the road construction crews, and that kind of work is sure to ruin my manicure. But if I miss one more mortgage payment, they'll foreclose on my condo and I'll end up on a street corner hawking designer cuff links for a night in a cheap motel."

But then it hit him. "Wait a minute . . . I've got it! I know exactly what I can do so that when I'm out of work, I'll at least have a decent place to stay. People will be begging to put me up in their spare room."

So he picked up his phone and started dialing. He called everyone with an outstanding loan to the dealership. "So, Mrs. Jones, how much did you owe on that Honda of yours? $14,000? Whew! Seeing how I like you and you're such a wonderful customer, let's just make it $10,000. No problem at all, just a stroke of the key." "Mr. Montague, what's still left on that new pickup truck? $30,000? Let's call it $20,000, just between you and me." "Mr. Casey, how much did we say for those flashy gold-speckled hubcaps? $11,000? Let's make it $6,000 and I'll even throw in a new GPS."

When the owner finally arrived from New York City and took a look at the books, he saw immediately what his manager had done. But what could he do about it? If he called all these people and bumped the prices back up, the bad publicity would probably cost him even more than the direct losses. So he called the manager into the office, leaned across the desk, and declared, "My oily friend, I have to commend you for some shrewd maneuvering. Don't get me wrong—you're a complete and utter slimeball, and you're definitely fired. But I think you have a bright future ahead of you."

Jesus concludes his story, "The slick car salespeople of the world are a lot more clever at dealing with their peers than most people of faith are. So I tell you, take a lesson. Use your worldly wealth to make friends for yourselves so that when it's gone, you will be welcomed into eternal homes."

* * * * *

Are you baffled yet? Vaguely repulsed? The subversion of expectation involved in this particular parable transcends time and culture. The manager's behavior is not just unethical and sleazy but probably jail-able. Yet Jesus elevates this man as an example to his followers! How can this be?

Jesus uses the story of this loathsome manager to make a very particular point. The key to unlocking the parable lies in recognizing what the manager is being commended for. The owner does not commend him for his waste of resources, or for his dishonesty, or for finding a way to brazenly cheat the system. The manager is commended in this story for one and only one character quality: he's shrewd. More specifically, he's a very shrewd investor.

This manager, sketchy though he may be, is a man who has read the signs of the times. He knows exactly what future is coming. He perceives that he's about to experience a rather dramatic change in circumstance. In a few more days, his Armani silk ties are going to be totally worthless to him. By this time next week, all that's really going to matter are his relationships, his connections, who is actually glad to see him when he comes down the road. So he seizes the moment he has to go all in on the stock he knows is rising.

In 1938 a comic book went on sale that featured a guy running around in blue tights with an *S* emblazoned across his chest. The purchase price was just ten cents a copy. A copy of the same issue introducing Superman more recently sold for $3.2 million. It's not exactly rocket science—if you know a stock is about to spike, you definitely buy it. The reason there aren't more rich people is the difficulty in predicting where and when the value will go up. When the *Death of Superman* issue was published in 1993, people snatched up copies, dreaming of riches. Today that particular issue sells for only around two dollars. That's the thing about investing—it tends to work best when you're investing in something the rest of the world has overlooked, perceiving value somewhere no one else has noticed it.

Jesus happens to be an excellent investment advisor. Being divine, he's got a pretty good grasp of what the future holds, of where the cosmic economy is going. And he's willing to give his followers the inside track.

The global economy, according to Jesus, is built on one giant bubble. Everything you build or buy, everything you store in barns or banks, everything you invest in real estate or spend on cars and home expansions—the moment you take your last breath, all that plummets in worth to zero. All your currency expires at the gates of God's new world. In the kingdom of heaven coming soon, all your cash is just scratch paper and your gold is merely paving stone.

But, Jesus teaches, there is one thing that makes it over the threshold to eternity and into the new world beyond—the people you invested in, the mercy you spent that money on. The only currency that transfers into Jesus' new world is that which has already been converted into relationships. "Use your worldly wealth to make friends for yourselves," he advises in Luke 16. Because when the cosmic scales are reset soon, it will not matter what you have; it will only matter whom you know, and who knows you.

In this parable, Jesus speaks of relationships in general as the carryover into his new world. But elsewhere in Luke's gospel, Jesus gets much more specific about which relationships in particular he has in mind. Shortly before the parable in Luke 16, Jesus is attending a party brimming with A-list guests, and he turns to his host and suddenly says,

> When you host a lunch or dinner, don't invite your friends, your brothers and sisters, your relatives, or rich neighbors. If you

do, they will invite you in return and that will be your reward. Instead, when you give a banquet, invite the poor, crippled, lame, and blind. And you will be blessed because they can't repay you. Instead, you will be repaid when the just are resurrected. (Luke 14:12-14)

With this prior teaching in mind, it becomes evident that when Jesus says "Use your worldly wealth to make friends," he's not talking about simply swapping favors with your buddies or going out to lunch after church with your usual crew. It's not wining and dining your man crush in hopes he'll decide you're awesome and invite you to join him at CrossFit. As Jesus points out elsewhere, loving those who love you, doing good to those who do good to you, might feel all warm and fuzzy, but it's not particularly to your credit (Luke 7:32-34). Even mafia dons and dictators do that, and sleep well at night. The people Jesus has in mind are given a particular definition—the poor, the crippled, the lame, the blind, those who cannot repay you or return the favor. These, Jesus says, whose worth has thus far been overlooked by the world, are the ones whose relationship will prove priceless.

Note that Jesus speaks of actual friendship, not just charity donation slips. He's very much talking about money, but he's also talking about something so much bigger. He's talking about life lived, and money spent, in ways that totally transform the whole field of our social connections and deepest relational investments.

Jesus has bypassed the usual religious guilt and obligation to open a conversation on money that begins with a whole different premise: spend smart. "Be shrewd investors," he says. "Seize the moment while you have it to convert your currency. Whatever resources you invest, many or few, spend them investing in the only stock that's rising: relationship—especially, especially with those less privileged than you. If you do, when the money's gone, there'll be a line at heaven's gates, waiting to welcome you home, and God will be eager to entrust you with more—true riches of a kind you haven't even dreamed of yet."

21

THE ATTIC BOX
The Epistles

Imagine you're cleaning out your grandmother's attic. Beneath fifty years' worth of saved butter-cookie tins (because, well, you just never know . . .) you find a box of yellowed letters from a great-grandfather you never met. Chances are none of these letters contains a list: Ten Things to Know about Me. Letters, after all, are written to particular people on specific occasions, assuming certain shared relational knowledge and communicating whatever's relevant to the moment. However, frequent references to the bank might suggest that your great-grandfather had money problems. The tenor of his advice could lead you to conclude that the recipient had suffered the loss of a loved one. Piecing together the clues, a picture begins to emerge of your great-grandfather's worldview, values, priorities, and relationships, as well as those of other significant people in his life.

After the four gospels and Acts, the rest of the New Testament is essentially a box of letters, written by leaders in the early Christian movement. Some, like 1 & 2 Timothy and Philemon, are addressed to individuals. Others, like 1 & 2 Corinthians and Philippians, are addressed to churches.

Like our imaginary attic letters, these letters (called "epistles") are occasioned documents, written in response to events in the recipients' own lives. They address actual questions and conflicts that are arising, correct mistaken teachings, and offer counsel on action to be taken in response to current affairs.

Reading an epistle isn't unlike eavesdropping on a roommate's phone call. You hear one-half of a two-way conversation: "Tell Jesse you're through!" your roommate commands. You have the answer, but your job as interpreter is to work backward to the questions. Is Jesse a boyfriend or a boss? Did he make a habit of stealing coworkers' ideas without giving proper credit? Did he lose his friend's beloved ferret in a locked room while she was on vacation? (Trust me: it happens.) Like a detective, you read with an eye for details that will help you begin to reconstruct, as much as possible, the situation to which the letter responds.

The situations the epistles address evoke responses that are both theological and practical. On the theological front, the writers of the epistles are seeking to help their communities comprehend the significance of Jesus and the seismic events of his death and resurrection. They do not address topics systematically, as in "An A to Z Guide to Everything Jesus." Rather, they take up topics as questions and controversies arise and prompt clarification.

In the biblical canon, the Gospels contribute to the broader conversation around Jesus' significance by describing Jesus' teachings, activities, and the events surrounding his trial, execution, and resurrection. However, by and large the Gospels do not venture into extended explanations about how these pieces fit together and add up to a new kind of picture of God, the people of faith, and the future of the world.

This critical integrative work is what the Epistles take up. The Letters add to the Gospels a crucial next level of understanding about what actually happened in Jesus and what exactly it all means. Their work is indispensable in beginning to unwrap the cosmic significance of the events that had taken place and to explain what Jesus' followers had learned about his identity. They discuss how the past looks different in light of Jesus' revelation of God, how our present reality has changed because of the freedom Jesus offers, how our future expectations have been altered because of the new world he inaugurates.

The larger theological truths established by the letter writers are then worked out in their practical implications for everyday life. Many of the letters notably change tone in their later portions as they shift from theological insight to behavioral application. At first glance, these instructional sections might look much like the Old Testament Law, laying out long lists of obligatory dos and don'ts. But Paul, the leader who wrote the largest portion of the Bible's epistles, insists that he is not simply replacing one legal code with a new, updated Christian one.

For Paul, Jesus laid the foundation for Christians. By his life, Jesus demonstrated who God is and what God wants. By his death and resurrection, Jesus broke us free from the powers of evil and of deep soul "stuckness," which kept us from responding. By sending the Spirit, Jesus equipped us with the resources we need to finally begin to really live the dreams of God.

The Old Testament Law, Paul explains in his letter to the Galatians, was like a guardian given charge of minors. But now those who belong to Jesus have become grown-up sons and daughters of God. They are no longer governed by the rule code necessary for children. ("Do not shove your brother in the dryer! Do I really have to say this? Not the washing machine either! That was supposed to be implied.") Instead, they are governed by God's Spirit, who is forming Jesus' mind within them so they begin to desire and to act from inner alignment with God's desires.

What we find in the Epistles, therefore, is not so much a new legal code as a series of exercises in what you might call "inspired improvisation."[1] For the first Christians, the question had suddenly gotten much bigger than "What does the Law require of us?" Now the question involved in each new situation was something more like "Who is Jesus, and what does it look like in this situation to live in light of him?" In an improv sketch, the scene unfolds within specific parameters assigned beforehand—for example, "Speak only using rap song lyrics." In the case of the early Christians, the designated parameters are "Act in ways consistent with Jesus' character and mission." But within these parameters, the actors play the scene creatively and responsively without a script dictating every detail of what happens next.

This manner of thinking took the church well off the old, well-marked map of the Law and into a startling freedom. In this sense, the epistles are like journals of early explorers who are charting new lands. In the Epistles we watch in real time while the church explores the significance of Jesus for a thousand different, complex, constantly changing situations: When Gentiles start believing in Jesus, do they have to get circumcised like Jews? (And should we mention this before or after they sign up for the membership class?) What does marriage or singleness look like for Christians? What qualifies someone to be a leader, and what do you do if your leaders get overloaded? How do Jesus followers relate to government when it is hostile to them? How about when it is not? How should the church respond when one Christian sues another?

In the city of Corinth, for one, Christians have been bringing their dinner to church. Since this is a church with great economic disparity, this means that while some wealthy members sit around munching sushi all afternoon, others stumble in late, after a long day's labor, and have nothing to eat at all. Now, to the best of our knowledge, Jesus never sat his disciples down for a conversation on the ethics of potlucks or brown-bag lunches. However, he did leave his disciples the tradition of a sacred meal, called the Lord's Supper, in which he instructed them to share bread and wine as symbols of his own body and blood, which are freely given for them. Every time they eat this meal in the future, he tells them, they will broadcast the story of his death (1 Corinthians 11:26).

Paul points out to the Corinthians the glaring inconsistency between Jesus' self-giving posture and their own. Every time they eat this way—selfishly, indifferent to the needs of one another—they demonstrate how little they've understood about who Jesus is. In fact, their meal actually broadcasts a distorted picture of what Jesus died for. Paul's practical conclusion? When the community of Jesus gathers, they should wait for one another and eat together in a way that accurately represents the self-giving posture of the one to whom they all together belong.

What Paul has done here is take an imagination inspired and formed by the life, death, and resurrection of Jesus and apply it to a question Jesus never directly discussed. He steers the Corinthian Christians toward an attitude and practice that aligns with Jesus' own character. The specific dilemma Paul addresses in 1 Corinthians 11:17-34 might be particular to the cultural habits of first-century Corinth, but in the way that he addresses it, Paul models in a larger sense the practice of Christian improvisation, demonstrating what it looks like to move from a truth *about* Jesus to a truth about what it means to *live in light of him.*

These are just a few of the questions that come up in the early church, requiring Jesus-shaped imagination for Spirit-guided improvisation. As you might guess, the answers are complicated and not without controversy. Churches quickly begin to share Paul's letters with each other, as it turns out that reading their neighbors' mail helps other Christian communities imagine what it means to view their own unique situations through the lens of Jesus.

What is happening in the Epistles is that the writers are clarifying larger theological truths about Jesus, his nature, and his character, which then interact with specific cultural or situational contexts to suggest particular behavioral or practical responses. The theological truths are universal, but as they interact with local contexts, different responses might be required. Not every community will conduct their meals in exactly the same way as Corinth. Each culture has its own customs around eating and its own indicators of social division. Carry-in dinners, food trucks, catering, and a communal cast iron pot are very different ways of feasting together, each of which raises unique kinds of questions. But in every case, Christian communities are called, like Corinth, to establish a pattern of eating together that reflects the truth that in Jesus, formerly disparate individuals have become one body in which the need of one is the concern of all.

Keep in mind as you read an epistle that letters are typically meant to be read in a single sitting, not like a thought-a-day calendar. The writer, sitting at a table before a piece of parchment, is following an internal flow of logic from one topic to the next. When you read a letter in small pieces with hours or days between them, it's easy to lose the flow of the argument or miss the themes that bind it together. Whenever possible, it's helpful to read straight through a letter in one go. Watch for words or images that come up frequently—these often provide clues about the letter's central themes. You might even try paraphrasing sections in your own words as you go along, which helps you hear how the argument is progressing.

Pay special attention to connecting words like *therefore* and *however*. These sorts of words indicate how one part of the argument relates to what comes next. Ephesians 4:25 says, "*Therefore*, after you have gotten rid of lying, each of you must tell the truth to your neighbor" (emphasis mine). If you want to know *why* Paul believes it's so crucial to get rid of lying, you have to trace the *therefore* backward to find the reason for this statement. In this case, the reason appears a few verses earlier (in 4:21)—"You were taught how the truth is in Jesus." In other words, the only appropriate response to seeing the truth fully disclosed in Jesus is to become people marked by the practice of deep and reliable truthfulness.

Be cautious around the italicized headings your Bible might use to divide epistles into sections. These headings are inserted by modern editors who are trying to help you quickly identify different topical sections, and they are not a problem in themselves. However, they often have the unfortunate side effect of artificially breaking up a fluid conversation and making the logic of movement from one thought to the next more difficult to see. It's also worth recalling that the headings themselves are an interpretation, reflecting the editor's decisions of what themes or connections to highlight. In some cases, changing the location or wording of a heading could significantly influence the way you hear the passage.[2] It's a good practice to deliberately read *through* the headings, making sure you observe how one paragraph connects with what comes next.

22

BACKSTAGE PASSES
Apocalyptic Literature

Every summer at the box office, the world ends in a dozen ways: meteor strike, nuclear war, climate disaster, global pandemic, robot uprising. In the parlance of Hollywood, "apocalypse" has become shorthand for the human twilight that is nigh when the zombie plague arrives to claim everything. But the term *apocalypse* does not itself mean "cataclysmic end of everything" but rather "revelation" or "unveiling." Apocalyptic literature in the Bible is a genre composed by people under pressure—oppressed, persecuted, or afraid. This literature peels back the curtain of the-world-as-we-know-it to show what's happening behind the scenes. It depicts a cosmic battle between Good and Evil in which the earth is contested territory and in which every act reveals in one way or another allegiance to a side.

The two books of the Bible that most clearly fall into the category of apocalypse are Revelation and the second half of Daniel. Apocalyptic books are generally hard to mistake thanks to their quite distinct features. (Dragons, for example, are a dead giveaway, as are any creatures with more than two heads). Reading an apocalypse bears resemblance to studying a piece of abstract modern art—it can be difficult to derive much meaning unless you have some training in how to view it or some understanding of what the artist is trying to accomplish.

One notable characteristic of apocalypses is their interest in symbols and symbolic numbers. Both Daniel and Revelation depict fantastical beasts rising out of the sea. Recall that the sea, for ancient people, was a symbol of chaos and destruction. These beasts, whomever and whatever they might symbolize, are unveiled in their true nature by their point of origin. The number seven was commonly used to represent perfection or completeness, and therefore it may not be a coincidence that the number 666—a trinity of incompleteness—is associated in Revelation with a figure trafficking in evil. The color white, in Roman culture, was a signal of victory. Apocalyptic literature is a case in which it may be especially valuable to draw on a study Bible or other reference book. Most of us need help understanding these sorts of key symbolic resonances that the original readers would have recognized.[1]

Another prominent feature of apocalypses is their tendency toward dualism. While the imagery is vivid, the apocalypse's world plays on a black-and-white TV. There is good, and there is evil, with no neutral ground between. Everyone must choose a side one way or the other, and that choice will have far-reaching future consequences, which the books spell out in detail.

Perhaps unsurprisingly for a genre of literature that took shape in times of crisis, apocalypses are not optimistic about the world. In quieter periods of history—or in insulated neighborhoods rarely touched by crime or poverty—we can sometimes convince ourselves that things are getting better, that if all of us work hard enough and learn to get along, we can usher in a golden age in which war is obsolete, droids do all the dishes and laundry, and pizza delivery boys live like kings. Apocalypses, however, offer a jolting reality check. History is not slowly progressing toward a human-made utopia; we're simply giving new shapes to our monsters. The mess we are in is far too great for us to solve; the only hope for the world is the direct intervention of God.

The most common mistake readers in every historical era have made interpreting biblical apocalypses, especially Revelation, is attempting to anchor the books' symbolic imagery in the preoccupations and politics of the moment. Christians in nearly every age of the church's history have been convinced that they and their generation were the culmination of the Bible's story. Starting from this mind-set, every symbol seems a thinly veiled reference to a present reality, person in the White House, geopolitical threat, or technological development.

To be clear, there's nothing wrong with attending to a book's resonances within current circumstances. In fact, this is key to recognizing an apocalypse's enduring relevance. But it's also important to understand that the symbolic imagery of an apocalypse is anchored in its own time. The kind of correspondences that might occur to us as we read—for example, that the wings of the marching locusts in Revelation 9 resemble the shape of helicopter blades—are interesting but ultimately arbitrary. Interpreting this way turns an apocalyptic book into a kind of Rorschach test, in which every generation ends up finding in the book an outline of its own darkest fears. This kind of reading might tell us much about ourselves, but it ultimately tells us little about what the book itself intends to convey. To avoid turning interpretation into an arbitrary game of word association, it's crucial that we begin by understanding how the images resonated in their original setting.

The same principle that applied in reading biblical poetry also applies to apocalypses—there is always a real danger of overinterpreting. We might set out to crack the code or try to load every word and image with a heavy freight of meaning. But not every detail of an apocalypse has major symbolic significance. Before you spend years building elaborate theories to explain the cosmic significance of a dragon's third nostril, it's worth considering whether some elements in the image might simply be there for artistic effect, adding brushstrokes of color that make the larger scene more vivid but don't necessarily imbue it with specific or individual symbolic meaning.

With an apocalypse, much like a work of art, the primary purpose is found in the emotional impact of the whole.[2] When you stand in front of a great painting, it causes you to feel something, or to see the world in a way that you didn't before. If you spend all your time scrutinizing the brushstrokes with a magnifying glass and never step back a bit, it's distinctly possible you'll never experience where the canvas meant to move you. You will have looked at the painting but not really seen it.

Interpreting an apocalypse well requires regular movements in and out. We zoom in to process any possible meaning of specific symbols; then we zoom out to take in the overall effect. Whatever we make of particular details, the key is to never lose sight of the book's central message: the victory of God over evil. All the symbols and imagery of apocalyptic literature support this one great reassurance: God's got this. They also direct the reader toward one central instruction: since you know who will win, choose the right side.

The book of Revelation has exerted a particularly powerful influence over the imagination of readers throughout the centuries. Some have concluded that this book provides a window to the future, a chronology of events that will precede the end of time. Others understand the book as primarily commenting on past events, reflecting the state of the Roman Empire somewhere around the end of the first century. It has often been assumed that Revelation's imagery specifically reflects a historical context of Christian persecution under an emperor such as Domitian. Some people argue that the effect of the book is primarily cathartic, letting otherwise powerless, suffering people get their feelings off their chest. Others, especially modern readers in the feminist or liberationist streams, view the book as inspiration to actively fight oppression.

It may not be necessary to choose only one correct approach. It is possible, for example, to identify some elements of the book that point forward in time and others that point backward in history. Multiple responses, including both relief and determination, may be reasonably evoked by the book's vivid imagery.

However, recent scholarship has challenged the common assumption that the context in which Revelation's story should be understood is one of widespread Christian persecution. Rather, the book appears to reflect a situation of localized but steadily increasing social and economic pressure on Jesus followers, an era in which persecution by the state is not yet widespread but is a possibility on the horizon.

The central concern of Revelation seems to be that Christians could be tempted to quietly compromise their core loyalty in order to avoid the prospect of loss, ostracization, suffering, and even death.

Babylon, the great enemy of Revelation, is a symbolic stand-in for Rome, in its corruptive wealth and power. But in a larger sense, Babylon also serves as a symbol for every human empire that consumes and co-opts consciences with promises of luxury and safety. Revelation calls God's people to "come out" of Babylon and its idolatry, to resist unholy alliances and conformity to the culture of the empire, which is antithetical to the rule of the God to whom they have promised allegiance. The symbolism of Revelation is rooted in the concrete historical realities of its time, and also wildly transcends them. Its message implicates both empires of the past and empires still to come.

In many ways, Revelation is a deeply Old Testament book. Its imagery borrows substantially from the biblical prophets Isaiah, Ezekiel, Joel, Jeremiah, and especially the Bible's other apocalyptic text, Daniel. One useful thing to watch for is how this imagery is picked up, adapted, or transformed to apply old words to new settings.

It is tempting to try to construct a chronological sequence of events in Revelation. However, the story that Revelation tells does not progress in a straightforward, linear fashion but rather proceeds in a kind of spiral movement. The book may circle around an event multiple times, applying different imagery to reinforce the same truths—a bit like a musical exercise in theme and variations. The aim of Revelation is not to map out a precise timeline of events but rather to expose the true shape of reality.

Revelation moves back and forth between symbolic depictions of events happening on earth and glimpses of behind-the-scenes heavenly realities. It assumes the two perspectives are integrally connected—historical events play out the twists and turns of an unseen spiritual struggle. Ordinary acts of compromise or resistance reflect choices of allegiance in a battle with cosmic stakes. Behind human forces lie spiritual powers in open rebellion against God. It's as if we've been handed a special pair of goggles that give us power to see a dimension of reality that would otherwise remain invisible to us.

In Revelation, we are given a glimpse of where history ultimately leads, where the cosmic struggle ends. Despite any appearance to the contrary, God remains in control, and the victory belongs to the Lamb who was slain—namely, Jesus. We participate in his victory by offering Jesus our allegiance, by resisting the seductions of empire, and by embracing the counterintuitive truth that the power that turns history has been revealed in the shape of a cross.

23

THE HEAVYWEIGHT
The Difference Jesus Makes

By this point it has probably become quite clear that the sixty-six books that make up the Bible each tell their portion of the story in a radically different voice. Reading an apocalypse with the techniques you use to interpret the proverbs is like eating a smoothie with the fork that worked on your steak—likely to end with frustration and very little fruit. But even if you've mastered the proper tools for every genre, you could discover as you read that a challenge begins to emerge. It's as if someone's taken Monopoly, Risk, and Settlers of Catan and dumped them together. You might find yourself looking at the board and wondering if all the pieces even belong to the same game. All the parts just don't seem to fit together the way you would expect.

In the story of Exodus, God introduces God's self to the Israelites as the one who heeds the cries of the oppressed. Yet neither the Old Testament nor the New Testament explicitly condemns slavery. Paul tells the Galatians that in Christ there is no "male and female" (Galatians 3:28), but in Leviticus the life of a woman is monetarily quantified at roughly half that of a man (Leviticus 27:1-7). In Genesis, God rains fire on the cities of Sodom and Gomorrah for their inhospitality to strangers (Genesis 19), but in Luke, Jesus sternly rebukes his disciples for suggesting the same punishment for a village that commits a similar offense (Luke 9:51-55). Not only do these statements appear in tension with each other, but that tension seems to carry over into the very character of God. The question we're left with is whether there is any larger ordering principle that can help us determine how the Bible's seemingly mismatched pieces actually relate to each other.

One possible way to answer this question is to simply assume that every statement in the Bible possesses equal authoritative weight. If a topic like violence, or judgment, or gender is addressed by Leviticus and Matthew and 2 Peter, each book places a pound on the scales. The Bible's authoritative word on the subject at hand is whatever the balance of these contributions turns out to be.

In this view, we discover what God is like through a straightforward process of biblical addition. The compassionate side of the divine encountered in Jesus is added together with Joshua's portrait of a God who commands the slaughter of cities. The sum of all the pieces, disparate as they seem, then composes the authoritative biblical revelation of God's character. Parameters for behavior as people of faith is decided similarly. The New Testament's teachings about love for enemies (Matthew 5:38-48) are added to the story of Jael, who drives a stake through Sisera's head (Judges 4). The proper course of action in any given situation presumably lies somewhere along this rather wide continuum of possibilities.

This seems like an intuitively reasonable approach. After all, all these stories and statements are contained in the same holy book, which Christians proclaim as "God-breathed."

The difficulty with this theory lies in execution, in figuring out how to combine portraits that seem disparate at best, and even contradictory. It's like adding together kiwis and kale, Picasso and Monet—it's hard to even envision what such a combination might entail. But even more importantly, another question remains: Does this approach of pure addition accurately reflect the Bible's own instructions as to how it should be read?

To suggest that all Scripture is inspired is to claim that God has things to say in every part of it. However, it does not follow that God speaks in exactly the same *way* in every piece. Truth be told, the strongest claims that the Bible makes concern not its own nature but that of Jesus himself. Jesus tells his disciples, "Whoever has seen me has seen the Father" (John 14:9). Paul describes Jesus as "the image of the invisible God" and boldly declares that "all the fullness of God was pleased to live in him" (Colossians 1:15, 19). Here we find the Bible's own take on an ordering principle for Scripture: Jesus is the very picture of God.

The trouble with an approach to biblical interpretation that takes the truth to be simply a matter of arithmetic (Old Testament God + Jesus = the reality of God and God's desires) is that any equation that qualifies Jesus, well, simply isn't biblical. According to the Bible itself, Jesus is the fullness of God's revelation—no qualifications, nothing concealed. He is the way God is encountered and known. He is the picture of human life as it is meant to be lived. He is the standard by which all truth is measured. He is the one who was with God from the beginning. He is God's Word made flesh (John 1:1-18)—the whole Word, not just a few of its friendlier pages. He is the definitive expression of God's heart and desires.

What this really means is that the Bible has a clear center. The Bible is a solar system in which every piece orbits a single radiating Star. Some planets may orbit closely and others at further remove, but all of them trace a path of meaning by their relationship to Christ. The author of Hebrews describes it this way: "In the past, God spoke through the prophets to our ancestors in many times and many ways. In these final days, though, he spoke to us through a Son. . . . The Son is the light of God's glory and the imprint of God's being. He maintains everything with his powerful message" (Hebrews 1:1-3). In other words, what we have seen in Jesus surpasses in clarity and brilliance everything that came before. They are the candle, but he is the sun. They are the echo, but he is the originating call.

The truth is, when you read almost any book, not every page has equal weight. When you know how a story ends, it changes how you understand all the earlier chapters. In a murder mystery, for example, when you finally learn who committed the crime, all the evidence previously uncovered finds its proper place. Once you know whom the story was pointing to, you finally possess the interpretive key to unlocking details that previously were just perplexing or might have even left you scrambling down false trails.

In Jesus, we've been handed the interpretive key to God's whole revelation. We've finally learned where the story was always pointing. Equipped with this newfound knowledge, we are in a position to sort the true trails from the false ones and to understand the past details in their proper light.

In the Jewish tradition of which Jesus and his first disciples were members, the authority of Scripture was not treated as flat, equal in all parts. The Prophets and wisdom Writings were important, but the Torah, the Law (the first five books of the Christian Old Testament) was viewed as the center of authority.[1] Jesus, for Christians, is the new Torah. He is the heavyweight who tips every set of scales he steps on decisively in his own direction. Everything in the Bible either moves toward him or flows out of him.

You might say that interpreting the Bible is a little like approaching a pile of brightly colored Legos. It isn't immediately obvious how all the disconnected pieces fit together. Left to our own devices, we could combine them to make almost any shape we wish. There would be no way to argue that one arrangement is better than any other. But Jesus is the picture on the front of the box that shows us what the outcome looks like when we're putting the pieces together as they were designed—forming, say, a ship instead of a tank, or a T. rex, or a helicopter.

In Jesus' teachings, in his life, death, and resurrection, we get the authoritative blueprint for how God actually intends the pieces of Scripture to interlock. If we want to know who God is and what God desires, if we want to know who we're called to be as humans, we start with Jesus himself.

24

A SATURDAY'S STROLL
How Jesus Read

I f Jesus is the center of authority for Christians, the defining revelation of both God and true humanity, then if we want to learn how to interpret our Scriptures, it seems reasonable to ask how Jesus read his. In fact, Jesus' approach to scriptural interpretation was a source of conflict and controversy in his ministry—especially in his relationships with religious professionals who did interpretation for a living.

One thing Jesus clearly taught is that all Scripture, interpreted rightly, finds its ultimate meaning in him. In the gospel of John, Jesus rebukes those who study the Old Testament Scriptures diligently, claiming eternal life is found in them, but who do not see those Scriptures as pointing toward him (John 5:38-40). They are the road sign, not the destination—the ad, not the event itself. In Luke, immediately after Jesus' resurrection, we find him on the road giving a lesson in biblical interpretation, explaining to a pair of oblivious disciples how every part of the Old Testament—the Law, the Prophets, the Psalms—finds fulfillment in him (Luke 24:13-27).

According to Jesus, it isn't enough to read these books for what their human authors had in mind; they also have to be read in light of the end toward which God was always shaping the story—namely, Jesus himself. Not every text in the Bible is *about* Jesus, but the full, God-intended meaning of every text can only be understood in *relationship* to him. If any part of the Bible is read in a way that does not ultimately move the reader toward Jesus, then, according to Jesus himself, something in interpretation has gone very wrong. When the back of the book says the answer is Jesus, anyone who ends up with a different result had better go back and check their math.

Jesus also explicitly asserts his own authority over Old Testament Scripture. He's famous for saying to his followers, "Here is what the Law says, but this is what I say to you . . ." In some cases, Jesus interprets the Law in ways that make the challenge even harder than its original statement—"Don't just avoid murdering your brother or sister; stop fantasizing about slashing their tires" (see Matthew 5:21-22); "Don't just keep your oath; be so reliable in your word that you don't have to swear to begin with" (see Matthew 5:33-37). Jesus' interpretation shifts the focus from simple behavior to the attitudes and character that underlie it.

In other cases, Jesus argues that parts of Scripture reflect movement along a trajectory but do not represent God's final word on a matter. For example, Jesus describes divorce as a concession Moses made because of people's unyielding hearts, but he goes on to explain that the Old Testament divorce law (Deuteronomy 24) does not tell the story of God's deepest desire, which is—and always was—faithful marriage for life (Mark 10:1-12). Exodus commands "an eye for an eye and a tooth for a tooth" in order to prevent escalating cycles of revenge (Exodus 21:23-25), but this law Jesus flat out overturns. God's people, he says, turn the other cheek when struck, and love their enemies as God loves God's (Matthew 5:38-48). By drawing a straight line from God's actions to ours, Jesus implicitly argues that the Law's prior instructions do not reflect the fullest and most accurate picture of God's character, which he himself is now making clear.

Jesus throws a wrench into the entire class of biblical purity laws—the set of codes that emphasized all the things that made those who ate or touched them "unfit" for God's holy presence. He affirms God's concern about purity but argues that the purity about which God really cares involves the heart rather than the hands, the tongue rather than the stomach (Mark 7:1-30). In fact, the whole logic of purity codes—that contact with the impure spreads impurity—is implicitly challenged by Jesus' own healing ministry. In Jesus, the direction of the flow reverses—when he touches the impure (or when they touch him), what is clean makes others clean (see Matthew 8:1-4).[1] Holiness turns out to be its own kind of contagion.

There is one set of laws that Jesus was particularly notorious for challenging—the Sabbath laws, which forbid the Jewish people from working on Saturdays. Jesus' relationship with the Sabbath laws, as well as the reactions of others to it, reveals a great deal about the difference in their respective approaches to biblical interpretation.

For the religious scholars of Jesus' day, the Law was a distillation of God's wisdom and desires. They sought to please God by keeping the commandments as precisely and carefully as possible. The trouble was, some laws are more specific than others. When the Law says "Do not give false testimony," that's pretty clear—you know when you are lying. A law about the Sabbath, on the other hand, is ambiguous. I mean, what exactly constitutes "work"? Does answering a few emails under the dinner table count? Is it okay to chop wood, as long as you don't get paid for it?

We all know how this game is played. You can have a rule that your dog isn't allowed on the furniture, but chances are it won't be long before she tests the details of this policy. Does it count as "being on the sofa" if she's lying on you while you are lying on the sofa? What if she just does some heavy leaning? What if she puts her front two legs on the sofa but keeps her back two on the floor? Humans and their best friends have much in common in this respect—ambiguity provides an opening ripe for exploitation.

To keep people from getting creative in their interpretation of the boundaries, the religious leaders liked to get a bit more specific. In the case of the Sabbath, they put together a detailed list clarifying the activities that counted as work—including drying, dyeing, tearing, writing, and erasing, to name just a few. They even declared that the farthest people could walk on the Sabbath without it becoming "work" was two thousand cubits (around one thousand yards).

The point of all these clarifications was to create a kind of fence around the Law, to keep people from even getting close to a violation. The problem was, it became very easy to lose the forest for the trees. Conversing with a biblical expert about interpreting Scripture, Jesus tells a story about a man who lies gravely injured beside the road (Luke 10:25-37). Instead of stopping to help him, the good, Scripture-loving people passed by. Why? Most likely because they were concerned about breaking the rules, like the one in which touching a dead body makes you religiously unclean. They are so determined to get the rules right that they cross over to the opposite side of the road to avoid any possible violation.

This story, known as the parable of the good Samaritan, is one of Jesus' most famous. What many readers miss is that this story is Jesus' contribution to a conversation about biblical interpretation. Just before telling this story, Jesus and the religious expert he's speaking with both agree that interpreting Scripture correctly means recognizing love of God and neighbor as its central calling (Luke 10:25-28). Jesus goes on to observe, by way of his parable, that if guarding what you see as the integrity of the scriptural rules keeps you, as a person of faith, from moving toward someone who is wounded, something has gone very wrong in the process of application.

In Matthew's version of this same teaching (Matthew 22:34-40), Jesus explains his interpretation of the Old Testament by saying that all the Law and all the Prophets are summed up by two key commands: "You must love the Lord your God with all your heart, with all your being, and with all your mind" and "You must love your neighbor as you love yourself." Recognizing these two commands as the heart of the Law doesn't make all the rest of it pointless. In fact, much harm can be done in the name of generic notions of "love" that do not take into account love's difficult demands of sacrifice, judgment, and truth. More specific biblical laws teach contextualized ways of living out these foundational callings of love for God and neighbor. They help demonstrate what true, authentic, God-shaped love looks like. Love is not cheating on your spouse. Love is keeping your word. Love is not moving the boundary stone an inch a day until you've claimed half your neighbor's yard (Deuteronomy 27:17).

The problem with many scriptural "experts" was that they'd missed the point—they'd gotten caught up building fences around the rules and had forgotten to ask what the purpose of the rules was to start with. When Jesus breaks rules, he does so with this larger intent in mind. On one occasion, he lets his hungry followers "work" on the Sabbath by harvesting grain to eat. On another, he infuriates religious experts by working on the Sabbath himself, healing non-life-threatening injuries. When questioned about this, Jesus explains, "The Sabbath was created for humans; humans weren't created for the Sabbath" (Mark 2:27).

What Jesus is really saying is that the Law is not arbitrary. The Sabbath laws were first given to newly freed slaves, people forced into rhythms of endless brickmaking. Among other things, the Sabbath practice offered new rhythms of rest. It honored their worth as more than cogs in an empire's wheels of production. Sabbath laws also guarded the interests of those who would be vulnerable in the Israelites' own future economy, ensuring they didn't build their own empire by doing to others what had once been done to them. This background is why Jesus can ask those criticizing him for healing on Saturday, "Is it legal on the Sabbath to do good or to do evil, to save life or to kill?" (Mark 3:4). One of the central purposes of the Sabbath had always been to ensure the flourishing of life. And for Jesus, the reason for a law matters. If the letter of the biblical law is being kept in a way that violates its true purpose, it is no longer a God-honoring practice but an exercise in missing the point.

The religious leaders are asking questions like "How far can we walk?" and "What activities can we get away with without it actually counting as work?" These are questions of

Sabbath rules. But when Jesus reads the same Old Testament passages, he asks what these laws are for, whom they were designed to protect, and how he can be faithful to their spirit by contributing to the promotion of life and the wholeness of the vulnerable.

These are questions of Sabbath imagination. As Mark 3:1-6 indicates, this interpretive revolution is a key part of what prompts the religious experts to go searching for a way to bring about Jesus' death.

25

READING CROSS-EYED
The Character of Jesus

We have seen by now that Jesus himself is the interpretive key to the Bible, the ordering principle that shows how the pieces properly align. In practice, this means that the outcome of our interpretation will depend a great deal on what we believe we've seen in Jesus himself.

Do an image search of Jesus, and you'll quickly discover how much conceptions vary. In one, Jesus sports inflated biceps and boxing gloves, spoiling for a fight. In another, he cuddles with a lamb and gazes upward with the long-lashed, guileless eyes of a baby unicorn. Who exactly is this man? Is he a warrior, a rebel, a provocateur? A lover, a teacher, a healer? In truth, Jesus is all these things in his own way, crafting whips and cradling children, breathing grace and bringing down rhetorical fire. Any account of the character of God revealed in Jesus must do justice to the complexity of Jesus himself as we see him in all four gospel accounts: forceful and gentle, humble and fearless, confrontational and compassionate.

But if Jesus is the center ring of Scripture, his story also has a center of its own. This bull's-eye that marks the very heart of the Bible's story is the cross itself.

All four gospels devote a wildly disproportionate amount of their narrative space to the events that surrounded the last week of Jesus' life. The church's earliest sermons, summarized in the book of Acts, maintain a laser focus on Jesus' execution and resurrection from the dead. Paul, writer of most of the epistles, describes belonging to Jesus as entailing participation with him in his dying and rising (see, for example, Romans 6:1-5 and Philippians 3:10-11). For the New Testament, Jesus is the very image of God, and the cross is the centerpiece of his revelation. The cross and resurrection are at the perihelion: the moment when we pass closest to the Sun. They are the place we get the clearest possible look of what God is about. So what exactly do we learn from these events, and how does that change the way we read the whole rest of the story?

One thing we certainly find in the cross is confirmation of God's mission. From the very beginning of the Bible, God expressed an intention to rescue creation from the hell we have made for ourselves. In the events of the exodus, the Old Testament's central story, God introduced God's self to the world as the Deliverer of the oppressed. In the cross, Jesus finally reveals the depth of God's commitment to ending our captivity—not just to human powers but to the forces of death and darkness and destruction themselves. The cross reveals God's mission to be a prison break.

It turns out that Jesus came into creation as a prisoner like the rest of us in order to break the whole world out. He's tearing the walls down as he goes so that no one can ever be trapped again. This is the motive behind everything God has ever done, the mission God has been plotting and planning and carefully executing, step by step, from the very start. The job will be done when the prison walls are ground into dust and the whole world is freed and healed and finally, fully alive.

But the cross isn't just a revelation of God's mission and motive—it's also a revelation of God's methods, how God intends to defeat evil and deliver the world from bondage. Here the story takes a surprising twist that nobody saw coming. Jesus doesn't take a battering ram to the prison walls. He doesn't dig a tunnel or set off an explosion. He doesn't start a riot or lead an uprising against evil's henchmen who are guarding the bars. Instead, he lets himself be led away to the execution chamber. He gives himself over for evil to do its worst. And when the deed is done and Jesus breathes his last, the earth beneath quakes and the walls collapse from the weight of their overreach. God's strategy for overthrowing cosmic forces of evil turns out to be the subversive power of self-sacrificial love.

Even those who knew Jesus best struggled to wrap their minds around this strategy. Of course they wanted God to fix the world; of course they wanted to be free. But they had their own ideas of what "fixing" and "freedom" really meant. The people of Israel at the time of Jesus belonged to an occupied nation. They were poor, and were heavily taxed by the oppressing power of Rome. Many expected Jesus to stage a political confrontation—rally the people, call legions of angels, take the government by storm—and then institute his own just and righteous rule on earth.

But Jesus did none of these things. He refused to threaten or coerce anyone to choose his more beautiful way. To do so, he understood, would be to concede to evil's terms and play straight into its hands. Instead, Jesus entered the prison and spoke the truth boldly. He bound up the wounds of the broken. He refused alliances based on fear and self-preservation. He spent his time with messed-up people from the wrong side of the tracks. He shared meals with his enemies. And at the end of the day, when all these gifts were forcefully rejected by guards and prisoners alike, he offered his own life willingly as a sacrifice in the place of his cellmates.

This is how evil's back was broken. This is the way the world was saved. This voluntary act of love, this freely given life, was the single thing the powers of darkness were not equipped to withstand. The cross dealt evil's deathblow.

This was not just a strange, one-off coincidence. The cross was not an accident. It was a strategy—a revelation of how true power is shaped, of how evil is overcome. There is only one force strong enough to break the grip of the forces of darkness, disrupt the systems of destruction, and shatter chains that hold lives in bondage: the power of relentless, indiscriminate, self-emptying love.

It turns out that, unbeknownst to us, the cross has two sides. While all the world sees is weakness and suffering, the flip side of the cross is resurrection. The way of the cross, paradoxically, is the way of unleashed power. What goes down in the way of Jesus also rises, as Jesus did, in the victorious power of God. This unbreakable principle was always hidden at the heart of reality. In Jesus it has finally been unveiled for the entire world to see, and believe.

If we want to know what God is like, we start with Jesus on the cross. If we want to know what power means, it looks like Jesus on the cross. If we want to know what God is working in the world to achieve, we find out on the cross. If we want to know God's strategy for how peace will be accomplished, on the cross it is revealed. To read the Bible in light of Jesus is to read it "cross-eyed": to have every page colored by this ultimate revelation of God.

And if we want to know who we are meant to be, the cross is the center of that too. After all, Jesus is not only the authoritative revelation of God but the authoritative picture of true humanity. Jesus says that anyone who wants to be his disciple must "take up their cross, and follow me" (Matthew 16:24). In other words, to follow Jesus means that his mission must become our mission, his methods our methods. There is no other way to journey with Jesus than to take up his mission of bearing God's evil-shattering, system-disrupting, soul-healing power to the world. And there is no way to participate in this mission except by using Jesus' chosen strategy of fearless, unshakable, self-sacrificing love.

To live in this way is to align ourselves with the true shape of the world. It might not pay off quickly. Truth be told, it might even get us dead sooner. But in making this choice to follow Jesus where he goes, whatever it costs, we claim a share in the cosmic victory won by the cross. In binding ourselves to the crucified Christ, we bind ourselves to the resurrection power to which the whole future belongs.

LIFE IN THE DARK
Reading Backward

For many readers, perhaps the most difficult aspect of biblical interpretation is deciding what to do with the many passages in the Bible that appear to promote extreme violence. Particularly troubling are stories that seem to implicate God in acts of wholesale slaughter that, if they occurred today, would probably be classifiable as acts of genocide. These sorts of stories provide a useful testing ground for considering what happens when we read the Bible backward, in light of Jesus and the cross.

"In the past," the author of Hebrews writes in the introduction to his book, "God spoke through the prophets to our ancestors in many times and many ways. In these final days, though, he spoke to us through a Son. . . . The Son is the light of God's glory and the imprint of God's being" (Hebrews 1:1-3). God didn't wake up to a blaring alarm on the day of the BCE–CE changeover and say, "You know, I think this is the day when I'll finally start talking to people." God had spoken to Abraham and Sarah, to Moses, to Joshua, to Deborah, to Ezekiel and Huldah, as well as to countless others whose names we don't know. The relationship between God and the people of Israel had been going on for a long time before Jesus arrived on the scene. The relationship between God and the world had been going on even longer.

History is littered with genuine divine encounters. God was always there, always communicating, always revealing truth. But the author of Hebrews posits that there is a qualitative difference between the past interactions and messengers, on the one hand, and the present word spoken in Jesus, on the other. There is simply no match for the clarity and certainty of what is heard in person from God's own lips.

In a sense, meeting Jesus is rather like donning a pair of glasses. Perhaps you weren't even aware that you needed glasses. Perhaps you thought you were seeing just fine. It turns out, however, that your vision was distorted by a kind of spiritual astigmatism, which left everything you viewed rather blurry. The same kind of astigmatism has afflicted everyone in the world for so long that none of us realized anything was wrong. We thought trees really were brown poles with green cotton candy on top. But in Jesus, for the first time, we're handed a pair of corrective lenses. God and the world suddenly snap into sharp focus.

Those of us reading the Bible today have a distinct advantage over even the greatest spiritual legends in Israel's history: we have the glasses they lacked. When we look back on stories and texts that do not share our advantaged position, the best place to begin is probably not by immediately meting out judgments. That's a little like being that friend who's already seen the movie and now looks down his nose at first-time viewers who can't comprehend every twist in the plot.

Before we read the Old Testament backward, however, we start by simply reading forward, trying to hear the stories on their own terms, as people at the time would have heard and experienced them. Our primary goal is not judgment but understanding. We ask ourselves, What was at stake for the people of God in this particular moment?

As a case study in reading forward, let's consider two prominent Old Testament stories: the conquest of the city of Jericho (Joshua 6) and the death of the firstborn children in Egypt (Exodus 11).

In Joshua, the Israelites, forty years ago freed from slavery to Pharaoh, are now finally poised to enter the land where God has promised they can settle and build a new life together under the rule of God. But if you read carefully, you might sense a significant question looming: How are the Israelites and their children going to stay loyal to God and God's distinctive vision while surrounded by neighbors who do not share their values or beliefs? How will they keep from adopting the same appetites and preoccupations and rhythms of life as everyone around them? The Israelites determine that the best course, the course that God commands, is to rid themselves of the neighbors entirely. After all, no one else can corrupt you if you're the only ones around.

The result is catastrophic devastation—the Israelites march into Jericho and cut down every man, woman, and infant in their path, all in the name of a holy God. But even as many of us reel in horror at their actions, a crucial question still lingers: How are they—how are we—to resist the seductions of idolatry, the temptation to adopt our neighbors' narratives of "normal" and lose sight of God's radically alternative call?

At the start of Exodus, the empire of Egypt is enriching itself on slave labor. Israelite babies are being slaughtered in defense of Egyptian privilege. In their suffering, the people cry out for help. A real question emerges: Does God hear the voices of the oppressed? Does God really care? The confrontation between God and Pharaoh unfolds in a series of plagues designed to demonstrate the superiority of God's power to the might and gods of Egypt. In the final plague, God declares that at midnight God will pass through the city, and the Egyptians wake up to find every firstborn child dead.

It's a horrifying scene, all the mothers of Egypt wailing in grief as Pharaoh finally lets the slaves go free. But even as many of us shudder at the slaughter, a crucial question remains: How does, or should, God respond to oppressive powers that hold people in captivity?

Reading each of these stories forward, we glimpse serious questions confronting the people of God—questions just as relevant today as they've ever been. But once we have heard the stories on their own terms and have seriously considered the very real question to which they serve as one response, we can put on our Jesus lenses and read them again. This time, reading *backward*, we ask how our answers to these questions might change in light of what we've seen in Jesus, the fullest revelation of God.

Reading the conquest stories backward, we might recall Jesus' command that his followers love their enemies, coupled with his bold claim that this is how God treats God's enemies (Matthew 5:43-48). We might note that Jesus heals the suffering daughter of a Canaanite (Matthew 15:21-28)—a member of the very people group the Israelites once slaughtered. More than that, Jesus even praises this Canaanite's tremendous faith—a startling counterpoint to the conquest's assumption that these Canaanites would inevitably be a source of Israel's corruption.

Perhaps of even more significance is the name of the commander who led Israel to victory during the conquest—Joshua. Although it's easy to miss in your English translation, this happens to be the exact same name the angel tells Joseph to give the baby whom Mary will bear—"You will call him Jesus (Yeshua)." Jesus is the second Joshua, born to a people under oppression. His name, which means "the Lord saves," sets up an expectation that he, like his famous forebear, will conquer the enemy and claim the land. But instead Jesus commands his followers to "put the sword back into its place" (see Matthew 26:51-54) and surrenders his own life to save the lives of his oppressors. The first Joshua's actions in the conquest must be understood backward, in light of the second Joshua's revelation of how salvation comes and whom it encompasses.

Reading the story of the death of Egypt's firstborns backward, we might first observe that Israelite families are protected from the death that claims the Egyptian children by placing the blood of a lamb over their doorframe. Seeing the blood, God "passes over" these households without harming them. The New Testament describes Jesus as the "Passover" Lamb, whose blood saves all those of any tribe who place themselves beneath it.

Exodus also asserts that the plague on Egypt reflects God's protection of Israel, who is called God's prized "firstborn" child (see Exodus 4:22; 11:4-7). Jesus himself enters the world as God's firstborn Son. But instead of killing the guilty in order to save God's precious firstborn, God surrenders the life of God's firstborn in order to save the guilty. In Jesus, the movement of Exodus is both recapitulated and completely reversed.

Jesus turns out to be the second Moses, come in God's name to bring a new exodus and lead the people into freedom. But from Jesus we learn that the true enemy is never another nation but rather the powers of sin and death we carry in ourselves. The only death that deliverance requires is God's own, and the freedom that death wins belongs to people from all nations who choose to walk in it.

Reading Israel's stories backward from Jesus and his revelation of God radically alters how we understand the significance of those stories. The people of Israel were always in real relationship with God. They spoke with God, they listened for God's voice, they experienced God's power in very real ways. But without the light of Jesus, they were living in the dark. In the dark it's still fully possible to see the outline of true shapes. But it's also possible on occasion to step on a slipper that turns out to be your sleeping cat.

The people of Israel saw many things incredibly well. But their own prophet Isaiah foretold that a day would come when "the people walking in darkness have seen a great light. On those living in a pitch-black land, light has dawned" (Isaiah 9:2). When Jesus comes, the sun finally rises (see Matthew 4:16; Luke 1:78-79; John 12:46). For the first time, the light clicks on. And suddenly, looking behind them, the people of Israel are able to see clearly what they only saw dimly before. In the light of Jesus, it is clear that they discerned many things well. However, it also becomes evident there were moments along the way when their senses may have deceived them, when what seemed to be one thing turned out, in the full light of day, to be rather another. There were times they drew lines between very real dots but connected them in the wrong order.

Recognizing this reality of life in the dark does not diminish the worth of the Old Testament. But it does mean that it has to be understood in terms of its proper place within the larger story. We now read its stories with the lights on, considering what Jesus has illuminated about the will of God. On occasion, where the Israelites once believed they had leashed an elephant, we may find a rhinoceros standing. Deliverance, conquest, kingdom, and power might turn out in the light of day to have different faces than we thought. This doesn't have to worry us, because God accounted for this all along.

God never expected Israel to have perfect eyesight in the dark. God was patient, and kept on pursuing them through the ups and downs, the miscalculations and the insights. God continued to speak to them and through them, imperfect vessels that they were. God was even humble enough to let God's name be bound to them and their choices, knowing all along that in fullness of time Jesus would come and bring the picture into focus.[1]

Each part of the story serves its intended purpose. The darkness sets the stage for the coming of Light. Now we read, worship, and live in the light of Jesus. In Christ, we've seen God and the world as they truly are.

STORYTIME

Unwrapping Genesis 6:5–9:29

IF GOD HADN'T tried it, we probably always would have wondered.

The world was a disaster in the old, familiar ways. Leaders lied and bankers stole. Lady Justice peeked under her blindfold. Nations built empires with mortar of blood. Husbands beat their wives. Mothers sold their children for a quick fix. Brother betrayed brother for the price of a boast. Even the scorched and stripped soil wept silently.

What do you do when the whole world's gone to hell? There's one obvious solution, both simple and satisfying. Gather all the good, decent, reasonable people, tuck them inside a reinforced bunker, then let loose the cannons of justice. Wipe the problem of evil right off the map.

Now, I know what you're going to say—this sounds a bit extreme. But think about it for a moment: terrorists, traffickers, slumlords, drug lords, pedophiles, corrupt politicians, hedge fund managers, Yankees fans—all of them, gone in an instant. What couldn't we—the good, decent, reasonable—accomplish with such a clean slate?

This is what happens in Genesis 6–9. God is sitting on the throne of heaven, watching in horror at what humans have made of the world, and then someone kicks an emu and it's the last straw. God has finally had enough. God uses God's skyview to locate the Clark Kent—the one good guy left, the righteous man in a generation—and sends him away on a round-the-world cruise while God stays home to clean house. God empties the oceans of heaven: ISIS—gone; dysfunctional Congress—out of there; trouble-making coworker who makes our life miserable—toast. Evil is annihilated. The fantasy is fulfilled.

We step outside our bunker-boat onto ground that's still sparkling with Lysol dew. And for a moment in time, things are perfect. Nobody's baking forbidden fruit pie. No one's polluting the river of life. It's just us and Noah—the righteous, blameless, faithful—planting the seeds of a bright new world. Welcome to Creation 2.0. Creation: The Righteous Edition.

Except wait a minute. Not so fast. What does Noah, paragon of decency, the world's one righteous man, do to celebrate the great triumph of Good? First he praises God (because he really is a good guy). Then he drinks himself into a self-satisfied stupor, passes out naked, and upon waking up hung over, curses the son with the misfortune to see him exposed.

You know that moment when a great fantasy suddenly springs a leak? This is it. It turns out that all that shame, violence, greed, and gluttony was not drowned with the monsters and Nephilim. It was a stowaway aboard the ark, carried aboard tucked away inside the vest of no less than the righteous, the blameless, the faithful, even Noah himself. We're confronted with a truth we'd prefer not to know. There's just one problem with defeating evil by deluge: it only works if no one's on the boat.

Now we've got a real dilemma. I mean, what's God to do? The world's still a disaster. The grand reboot seems doomed to fail. So God regroups and bravely picks a new human partner, a guy named Abraham. This is where the story starts to get strange. Because if God has a type, it's clearly Noah. God swipes right for blamelessness, faithfulness, the great man of a generation. Abraham is another story entirely. He's a middle-aged guy from Ur with no kids whose main hobby appears to be moving a lot. If Noah is the winner of the global talent search, Abraham is the guy you pick up at a truck stop.

God picks Abraham, seemingly at random, from the dysfunctional masses and says to him, "Here's the deal. I'm going to give you land, family, fame, influence. I'm going to make you a nation. I'm going to be so good to you that #blessedlikeAbe will be a thing someday. I'm going to bless you so much you won't be able to contain it, and it will spill over on everyone around you. In exchange, all I ask from you is this: show up and keep your hands open for the presents."

It's undeniably a great deal for Abraham, but it's hard to see how this is a solution for global catastrophe. But God's ways are mysterious and all that, so we can suspend judgment for a minute to see what happens.

What happens is that Abraham gathers up all these promises and sets off on a trip to Egypt. Now, here's the thing: it's not that Abraham is prejudiced. No way. It's just that everybody knows that bad stuff happens in Egyptian neighborhoods. So just as a precaution, to be sure no one kills him to steal his lady, Abraham asks his wife Sarah to lie for him and say that she's his sister. As it happens, Pharaoh takes a shine to her, marries her, and makes her "brother" Abraham a very rich man. Abraham gets a lot of free donkeys, while Sarah has to perform her "wifely duties." Meanwhile, Pharaoh has no clue anything is wrong until his whole household comes down with diseases. Pharaoh ultimately sends Sarah home and Abraham slinks out of Egypt, slightly ashamed of himself but also considerably more well-to-do than when he went in.

Just to be clear on what happened here: Abraham lied about his wife to protect himself and traded her in for camels, and all this was motivated by his apparent conviction that foreigners like Pharaoh and his people could have no honor. Okay, this guy's clearly no Clark Kent. But anyone can make a mistake, right? At least, thanks to God's intervention, Sarah's home and they're back on track.

Years pass, and God is on Abraham like white on rice. Abraham can't turn around without God being there, giving him gifts, making him promises. After a decade or two, Abraham is traveling again, this time in Gerar. And he thinks to himself, "You know, those Gerar peeps are almost as bad as Egyptians." He starts to get nervous. And next thing you know . . . he's asked his wife to lie and gotten her taken by the king once again. Exactly the same bone-headed move as before!

This time, though, the consequences are worse. It's not just Sarah who is at risk. Every woman in the palace suddenly goes barren, and the whole household is under threat of death—all because of Abraham. God intervenes with the king, rescues Sarah, and then gets right back to blessing Abraham.

You can be forgiven for wondering when this grand new plan of God's is going to kick in. What kind of story is this? What is God doing with a screw-up like this? And how is any of this an answer to the global mess?

The world was a disaster in the old, familiar ways. Leaders lied and bankers stole. Lady Justice peeked under her blindfold. Nations built empires with mortar of blood. Husbands beat their wives. Mothers sold their children for a quick fix. Brother betrayed brother for the price of a boast. Even the scorched and stripped soil wept silently.

Then along came Jesus, who declared: "God causes the sun to rise on the evil and on the good. God sends rain to fall on the righteous and on the unrighteous" (see Matthew 5:45). Behold, the revelation of God's grand new global strategy. So long ark and goodbye flood. Farewell Noah. The problem of evil is answered by . . . a shower of indiscriminate mercy.

Can we be honest with each other for a moment? Most of us know deep down that this is a terrible idea. The world's got real problems: nations testing nuclear weapons, clergy abusing power for sex, terrorists in subways and at concerts, polar bears drowning. Give us fire! Give us flood! Give us a holy tsunami! We need something huge, powerful, shocking, something that breaks the back of evil in a sudden wave of judgment. The power of rain to change the game by casting soft, persistent pearls of grace? We can't imagine a world healed like this, one drop at a time.

Yet Jesus proclaims it boldly: God is emptying the ark. No more "righteous," "blameless," "faithful"—God is calling out the lie, inviting all the culpable to come out under the open sky. To stand there with our heads thrown back, being showered by mercy. To drink it in. Let it run down our faces. Let it soak through our clothes and pool in our shoes. To remain in the rain until our wounds are soothed and our stains are cleansed. Until our vision clears and our thirst is quenched. To remain in the rain until our deserts bloom, and in the depths of our soil all things become new.

Truth be told, I've never met an unblemished Noah. Not a single one. But I do know lots of Abrahams. Chances are you're one. An average person somewhere on the spectrum between normally flawed and downright screwed up. A person who's made the same mistake more than once or twice. A person who's gotten scared or selfish and caused your share of wounds.

When someone decides to follow Jesus, there's a ritual Christians do where we dunk the new follower into a pool of water. This ritual, called baptism, is a reminder that God doesn't need Noahs, floating high and dry in an ark of righteousness. God is looking for ordinary Abrahams who will plunge themselves beneath a flood of Jesus' mercy.

You might ask yourself from time to time what difference it makes. Maybe you've made the same mistakes again, feel like the same person you always were, only wetter. But there's one small detail of Abraham's story that's often overlooked. The second time Abraham screws up, trades his wife, and brings disaster on a nation, God picks him up and sends him back to pray for those he's wounded (Genesis 20:17). And the entire household is healed because of Abraham's intervention, because Abraham had the courage to return to the site of his mistake and make the wrongs right. Despite what it may seem, something really is changing, one drop at a time. Slowly but surely, Abraham is becoming a vessel of God's healing waters.[1]

"God causes the sun to rise on the evil and on the good. God sends rain on the righteous and on the unrighteous." Jesus says his disciples are to be like the One they serve. We are to be the world's rainmakers, its showers of indiscriminate blessing. We are to rain so softly and steadily, so strongly and relentlessly, that hardened ground remembers how to drink. We rain mercy on the foreigners we fear. We rain mercy on those sitting across the political or ecclesial aisle. We rain mercy on the spouse we know doesn't deserve it tonight. We rain mercy on neighbors, rain mercy on coworkers. We rain mercy on friends and on enemies too.

The rainbow in the sky isn't just a promise; it's a declaration of strategy. There is hope for a broken world; there is an end to evil. And it comes when God's people learn to fall like rain with the Son's light shining through them.

PART III

BRINGING IT HOME

27

TELESCOPE DISSECTIONS
Reading for Transformation

Owning a Bible is rather like possessing a high-definition telescope.[1] In part 2 of this book we took the telescope apart, examining how the components work, asking what role each has to play in the function of the whole. But the purpose of having a telescope is not so we can spend the rest of our lives admiring the luminous nature of the lenses. A telescope exists to draw our eye through it to the vast universe it magnifies. Similarly, the Bible exists first and foremost not to be gazed *at* but to be gazed *through*: to draw its readers into awe and worship of God.

This might sound like stating the obvious, but it's not unusual for those newly introduced to the tools of interpretation to become excessively preoccupied with the telescope itself. More than a few students of the Bible have found themselves spending years unscrewing the device, analyzing the parts, holding them under a magnifying glass, without ever looking upward at the constellations they were designed to illuminate. I've talked to many people sitting amid a pile of disassembled screws and scopes and mounts who complain, "This stupid thing is broken! I don't see a thing when I look through it!" Well, yeah. Deconstructing a hamburger also doesn't make you full.

At this stage in the game, it's worth pausing for a moment to consider an all-important question: How do we deploy our interpretive tools so that we truly encounter the view and don't just find ourselves stuck in an endless analysis loop of the parts? To state the question even more plainly: How do we read the Bible so that we don't end up just parsing words but actually hear the living Voice addressing us through them?

People of faith have been grappling with this question for centuries, and it's become increasingly urgent as our tools of analysis have multiplied. It would be hubris in the extreme to imagine that encounter with God could be reduced to a formulaic equation (sunrise + coffee + Hillsong soundtrack + Instagram photo = divine revelation). There is, however, a kind of rhythm of reading we can bring to the Bible that helps keep the tools of interpretation in their proper place: as servants to the view rather than a distraction from it. The rhythm I'll describe here is not particularly new or novel but has been depicted in many related ways by Christian thinkers through the years. It sticks around, quite frankly, because it works.[2]

STEP ONE: **DOWNSHIFT**

Reading the Bible to hear God's voice requires a deliberate move away from our normal Internet-reading mode, in which we suck up information with the relentless efficiency of an industrial vacuum cleaner and forget it just as fast. When we open the Bible, we are entering another dimension in which the rules of our old world simply don't apply. Efficiency is irrelevant. Abstract information is worthless. In this universe, the words don't mean much until they sink beneath the skin and get pulled into the bloodstream.

Before we even crack the Bible's cover, we pause to shift ourselves into a new frame of mind. We remind ourselves that we have not come to the Bible to dissect, analyze, critique, or consume religious information. We haven't come to pack ammo into our cannons in hopes of blowing our neighbor's arguments out of the water. We have not come to be comfortable or have our biases confirmed. As much as possible, we release our agenda and hand control over to God. Then we simply settle ourselves into a posture of hospitality, receptivity, and listening.

STEP TWO: **READ**

For real. I mean it. Read. As in, actually-take-in-words-so-as-to-comprehend-their-meaning, not sweep-eyes-across-the-page-and-hope-to-learn-through-sheer-osmosis.

For those of us used to skimming media as fast as our fingers can swipe, it's a real trick sometimes to remember how to actually read. This is even truer if we have reason to think we already know the story in front of us. It's like the strip mall next to my apartment complex that I pass at least four times a day—it's all just so familiar, I don't have a blessed clue what's there.

The funny thing about listening for God as opposed to skimming for highlights is that God (like the proverbial devil) is often in the details. There are many creative methods you can use to engage your mind if you find concentration challenging—read the text out loud, copy it by hand, doodle the images, circle key terms, make a paraphrase. Whatever you do, just try to hear each word. Deliberately engage your imagination until a solid picture of the scene has formed in your mind.

STEP THREE: **EXPLORE**

On occasion, you might be simply reading along through Zephaniah when suddenly a few words jump off the page and God addresses you personally about a conflict you're having with a friend. This is one way the Bible sometimes works: the words on the page serve as a kind of open channel through which God calls directly.

But the Bible isn't only a kind of hearing aid that amplifies God's outside speech. The Bible is already full of communicated meaning; it itself *is* a form of address. Its own stated revelations of God and God's desires form the foundation and the testing ground for all we might sense God saying to us from beyond it. This is why it's important for us to hear as clearly as possible what God is speaking directly within Zephaniah's own thoughts and experiences.

This is the process for which part 2 of this book has sought to equip you. Spread the tools across the table and apply them as you're able. Explore the literary context, what's happening around the passage you read. Consider the historical context by using a study Bible, an online search, or a reference book you have on hand. Take into account what you've learned about genre and how this type of text communicates. Don't forget to factor in how the text may look different when read in the light of Jesus. This whole toolbox is designed to help us explore the possibilities of what God, through the text, may be pointing us toward.

The crucial point throughout this whole process is to keep your eye on the prize. You are not simply gathering information; you are listening for what God is saying to you through it. Imagine keeping one ear attuned down to the text and the other tipped upward. You're looking not just for what the words might mean generally but for where they touch down in the particularity of you and your own world, with an ultimate goal of acting in response. You are reading to be changed. This matter of orientation is a critical difference between using your tools to dissect the telescope and using the tools to put it together and then actually gaze through it.

STEP FOUR: **TALK. START WITH GOD.**

For many people, the practice of prayer often feels like being on a bad date. You're not sure what to say. There's a lot of awkward silence. You find yourself rehashing the same old topics—weather, the playoffs, your mom—for lack of a new idea. You're trying so hard to present yourself well, to find the perfect words, that everything feels stilted.

There's good news on this front: God's really not that into eloquence. It's honesty that gets God going. Whatever you think you hear in the biblical text, this is your starting topic for conversation. Simply talk to God about where you see the text overlap with your own life and world. Be real about where it challenges you, or upsets you, or stirs up longings. Also keep in mind that conversation and monologue are two different things. Pause on occasion to take a deep breath and listen for what God might say back to you. Take note of any words or images that flash through your mind as you listen.

STEP FIVE: **SHUT UP**

The Bible does not belong in the self-help section of the bookstore. It's a book that facilitates human transformation, but—much like the pull-up bar in my apartment that I occasionally dangle from futilely—the changes almost never come simply because one day we grit our teeth and try harder. When we prepare ourselves to read the Bible, we are opening a mine shaft into the depths of who we are, all the best parts and the untransformed worst. We can try to follow that mine for some distance, but the truth is, we'll spend a lot of time stubbing our toes in the dark and running into dead ends. The only one truly qualified for the most important deep-earth excavation is God.

There's a moment in the process when the best thing we can do is shut up and wait, just sit in the presence of God and let God do the transformative work underneath. At this stage, it's not your job to do anything at all. Just fix your attention on God as firmly as possible and let God do the heavy lifting. Don't worry about what you feel or what you don't feel, about whether or not you sense anything happening. This space is God's to do as God wishes. What happens here is not on you. Sometimes the most important changes are happening when we feel nothing at all.

STEP SIX: **LIVE**

Whatever you heard as you pondered and listened and talked, whatever glimpse you may have caught of God's vision for the world, whatever subtle tug of calling or conviction you sensed, it wasn't just there to enrich your mind—it was there to move your life. Reading the Bible without working it out is like eating without ever moving. It really doesn't matter how great the food is—if you don't use it to fuel action, it just ends up sitting there clogging your arteries. The more accustomed we become to inaction, the harder it becomes over time to actually hear and respond to the movement of God.

Tomorrow is the worst day to do anything about what you heard in the Bible. Words from God are not cellophane-wrapped Twinkies that can sit on the shelf for years on end and emerge tasting exactly the same.

Living words from God are like fresh bread. Their best moment is always right now.

WHY TO (PROBABLY) NOT PREACH NAKED
Introduction to Application

Interpretation is the art of discovering what the Bible *meant*. Application is the art of discerning what that message *means for me today*, how I'm meant to respond to it. It lies at the critical juncture between learning and lived response.

It would be nice if we could reduce our entire principle of application to a straightforward statement like "The Bible says it—therefore I'll do it." But we've had plenty of occasion by now to see why matters are more complex. To begin with, not every passage in the Bible comes out and issues a direct command to follow. In Isaiah 20, the prophet Isaiah takes up naked street preaching. Interesting as this sounds, it's not clear that the appropriate application to every person in every setting is to witness Isaiah's example and then go and do likewise.

Second, there are often significant differences between the circumstances facing people thousands of years ago and those we face today, and it isn't always immediately evident what a word to one might have to do with another.

The book of Acts, for example, depicts the early Christians in Jerusalem pooling their money and property and living from a "common purse" as a key part of their witness to Jesus (Acts 2:42-47; 4:32-37). If you attend a suburban church that draws thousands of commuters, the implications of directly transferring such a practice into your own highly mobile cultural setting sound complicated, to say the least.

Suppose I open my Bible one Tuesday morning and find myself reading the passage in Luke 18:18-30 where a rich ruler comes to Jesus and asks what he must do to obtain eternal life. This is a man who's got it all. To his credit, however, he seems to realize that "all" won't be worth much if the goods are only temporary. The one thing he's missing is . . . forever.

Jesus answers, "You know the commandments: Don't commit adultery. Don't murder. Don't steal. Don't give false testimony. Honor your father and mother." The man breathes a sigh of relief. He's got the Ten Commandments aced. He has never cheated on his wife, never lied under oath. He's even refrained from killing his mother-in-law's cat, who truth be told, has it coming.

But then Jesus adds, "There's one more thing. Sell everything you own and distribute the money to the poor. Then you will have treasure in heaven. And come, follow me."

Before we seek to apply any passage, we always start with the overall question of interpretation: What is the passage concerned with, and why? The interpretive tools we acquired in part 2 help us hear what the text is trying to say. As we listen, we concern ourselves not only with explicit commands, which may or may not be present as they are in this story, but with the portrait the text paints of God and with what it suggests about the contours of a flourishing, Christ-centered life.

It might be tempting to dismiss Jesus' directive to "sell everything" as pure hyperbole. However, the man's obvious devastation in the story seems to imply that he took Jesus quite literally. We have here a real command from Jesus to a man that he actually give up everything he owns.

But before you rush out to crash eBay or offload your car to pay for a ticket to eternal life, there's something else we might observe from the literary context—Jesus doesn't make this same command to everyone he calls. Many of Jesus' followers retained their property. Simon Peter, Jesus' right-hand man, had a home in Capernaum that Jesus used as a headquarters. Zacchaeus, another rich man whose story is told just a few lines later, gives up a mere half of his possessions for Jesus (Luke 19:8). The command to "sell everything" apparently does not extend literally to everyone.

There is, however, a second command that Jesus gives the rich man in the same breath as "Sell everything": "Come, follow me." This command, unlike the first, weaves through the Gospels as a continual refrain. It appears that the "one more thing" this man is missing, the one thing eternal life absolutely requires, is to follow Jesus himself. The trouble with wealth in this story is that it's a serious obstacle to that foundational act of following. Concern for making money, spending money, safeguarding money is keeping this man too distracted, or too busy, or too afraid to go all in with Jesus wherever he is headed.

Once the overall picture of interpretation is established and we've recognized the text's key concerns and insights within its own time and situation, we are ready to move on to the critical step of application: How does this text come home to me? The movement toward application begins when we consider where our world overlaps with the world of the text.

Figuring this out is an art more than a science, an exercise of imagination. "Doom to those going down to Egypt for help!" Isaiah 31:1 says. "They rely on horses, trust in chariots because they are many, and on riders because they are very strong. But they don't look to the holy one of Israel; they don't seek the Lord." At one point in their history, the Israelites were slaves to Egypt, but in the later years of Judah, they looked to Egypt as an ally, hoping the strength of its military would save them from the threat of larger empires looming to the east.

At first glance, this passage appears to have next to nothing to do with me. Were I to feel threatened by a neighbor, there are at least two calls I'd place before dialing up the Egyptian embassy. But when I hold the passage to the light and turn it around a bit, I might begin to see a broader theme emerging. The Judahites in this situation are under pressure, and the question is where they will look for help. I've been under serious pressure before. Where did I look for help? If I were in serious trouble now, how many phone calls would I make before I'd think to ask God to intervene? For that matter, what personal problem am I facing right now that I've worked from every angle—including an intimate chat with my local barista or hairstylist—and yet it's never even occurred to me to talk to God about? Rather like opening the child safety lock by turning the lid of the aspirin bottle until the tiny arrows meet, application emerges when you keep turning the text until some crucial detail of past and present aligns. Right there, at the click of alignment, the story opens up.

Turning the story of Luke 18 around in this fashion, I'm invited to consider my own relationship with money. In interpretive terms, it seems evident that Jesus is not saying every single person must sell everything they own. However, every single person must actually follow him, and doing that requires grappling with the myriad ways money can distract from or derail real obedience. Living as a disciple, according to this story, demands a radical divestment of anything—monetary or otherwise—that hinders a person from full participation in Jesus' mission.

I may not be rich, but I certainly have something. How exactly is my relationship with money—earning it, saving it, spending it, or just wishing for it—affecting my life? How much space is it occupying? Is my interaction with money moving me toward Jesus or away from him? There is no neutral. What other obstacles are keeping me from following Jesus fully? What would it look like for me to begin divesting myself of whatever it is that holds me back?

Before we rush out to act on any new insight we glean from a particular story, it's also worth considering the ways that insight may be nuanced, expanded, or qualified by other parts of the Bible. It's important not to rush toward this question too quickly. Our instinct often is to take what we find in a particular passage and immediately combine it with everything else we know the Bible says on the subject. I might read Jesus' command to "sell all your possessions" and start thinking of what Deuteronomy 28 says about God rewarding obedience with material goods. This might lead me to conclude that Jesus couldn't actually mean what he said, or perhaps that he meant to reward this man's sacrifice with a second house and an even bigger bank account.

The trouble with taking two disparate texts and immediately harmonizing them is that we usually end up missing the challenging nuance of each one. Maybe everyone isn't called to sell everything they own. But this man in Luke 18 certainly was. And that's worth taking seriously. This good, God-honoring man seems to be doing everything right, yet something about wealth is so problematic that he can't have it and Jesus too. Before we qualify the story or start composing a long footnote full of exclusion clauses, it's worth simply sitting in the story for a while, reflecting on what insight this particular text might suggest.

But once we've allowed ourselves to thoroughly feel the story's unique challenge, there is a place for considering the Bible's wider testimony. The Bible's word on complex subjects is itself often complex. Proverbs 10:19 declares, "With lots of words come wrongdoing, but the wise restrain their lips." If I read this verse on any given morning, it would appear to make a strong case for me keeping my mouth shut that day. However, the prophet Ezekiel is also told that if he stays silent about the words God has given him for his neighbors, God would hold him personally responsible for their blood (Ezekiel 33:1-9). The specific situation I am facing that day might require bold speech, or it might require disciplined silence.

Different situations call for different responses. Wearing a parka, scarf, and gloves is a great way to avoid pneumonia—unless you live in Arizona in July, in which case it's just a great way to die quickly. Sometimes faithfulness means speaking boldly. Sometimes it means sitting down and shutting up. Sometimes following Jesus demands selling everything. Sometimes it demands investing wisely. Applying the Bible's truth correctly in a given situation requires recognizing the range of insights on faithful practice that the Bible offers. Not every true word is the defining word for every situation.

Discernment is the term we use for the art of figuring out how to apply the right word at the right time.

One key factor to consider before taking any action relates to Jesus himself. Deuteronomy 19:21 says clearly, "Life for life, eye for eye, tooth for tooth, hand for hand, foot for foot." The application is fairly straightforward: if a coworker eats your cup-o-ramen today, you eat theirs tomorrow. But in Matthew 5:41, Jesus asserts a contradictory principle—if an oppressor eats your cup-o-ramen, give him your emergency bottom-drawer Snickers bar as well.[1] The application of Deuteronomy 19 has been overwritten by Jesus' interaction with it.

When we apply the Bible, we attend to the truth contained in the specific text we are reading. Our goal is to properly apply this insight, in all its particularity, to our everyday life. But as we do this, we also remain aware that every verse and story appears in the context of a larger book, which adds nuance and suggests the full range and limits of potentially faithful action. Wise application always keeps in view the contributions of this broader testimony.

29

YES, NO, BUT, MAYBE, SORT OF
Exploring the Biblical Dialogue

When we consider the Bible's broader testimony on a given subject, we may occasionally find ourselves baffled by the results. There are some questions on which the Bible speaks with overwhelming clarity. Themes like the sovereignty of God, God's call for holiness, and God's concern for the poor are threaded in one way or another through nearly every book of the Bible. The sheer consistency and prominence of such themes reveal them to be essential components of faith in the God of Israel, of Jesus.

But in other cases, when we set off to look for what the Bible communicates about a topic, we find ourselves navigating murkier waters. While God's commitment to the poor is as subtle as a Las Vegas billboard, the Bible's attitude toward wealth seems considerably more varied. Proverbs 10:22 boldly declares, "The Lord's blessing makes a person rich, and no trouble is added to it." Jesus tells a story in which people who are faithful with a few valuable coins are entrusted with even more (Matthew 25:14-30). Yet the prophet Habakkuk also complains that plenty of people get rich doing evil while trampling the good (Habakkuk 1:12-17). And Jesus also ominously declares, "How terrible for you who are rich, because you have already received your comfort" (Luke 6:24).

One important question in ancient Israel was how people of faith were to relate to those outside their ethnic tribe. Ezra commands the people to divorce their foreign wives immediately, with a speech strongly implying that intermarriage was the wickedest deed conceived since the first person thought to slide an empty milk carton back into the fridge. In sharp contrast, Genesis and Exodus depict Israelite heroes like Joseph and Moses successfully married to foreign women, who are largely portrayed positively. The book of Ruth even tells the story of a noble foreigner who becomes the great-grandmother of Israel's greatest king.

The New Testament books of Acts and Revelation both explore the Christian relationship to government. Both books share a keen awareness of the way the state can set itself up as a rival to God. However, Acts generally minimizes the threat that Christianity poses to the Roman Empire and goes out of its way to emphasize how public disturbances associated with Christians were actually incited by other parties (see Acts 17:5; 19:37). Sergius Paulus, a significant government official, even converts (Acts 13:6-12). Revelation, on the other hand, is much more overtly focused on the opposition between Christianity and the empire. Kings and rulers are portrayed as allied with evil and ripe for terrible judgment.

The principle we've already explored of reading texts backward from Jesus might shed light on some of these questions, but it is far from being able to resolve all of them. On some points, tension even seems to exist between various teachings of Jesus himself. If God's character doesn't change, and if the individual authors of the Bible are all inspired by God, it is rather perplexing that on so many topics the biblical text seems to point in multiple directions at once.

Before we throw up our hands in despair or conclude that the Bible is not inspired or God just isn't coherent, there are a couple of things to keep in mind. First, many matters in life are just complicated. Money is neither an unmitigated good nor an absolute evil. Divorce is not God's ideal for marriage, but neither is it the worst thing that can happen between two people. Some questions possess answers that are simple and straightforward, while others require responses that are as complex and nuanced as the situations they address. If a mathematician plotting the trajectory of a rocket launch comes back with the answer "2," we might justifiably wonder if she has accounted for all factors.

Second, the greatest and most encompassing truths often exist in rigorous tension where two opposing goods pull against each other. For example, the balance of justice and mercy, or of grace and accountability, cannot be summed up in a neat and tightly packaged sentence. Telling the truth about justice or the truth about mercy requires a tension line continuously held taut between them. To release the tension would be to release the truth.

To life's most complex questions, the Bible's answer is sometimes not just yes or no but rather "Yes and . . ." or "Yes, sort of . . ." or "No, but . . ." This does not mean the Bible is being wishy-washy. Wisdom's face is simply full of wrinkles. Some questions require layered and nuanced responses. Truth often exists in vital tensions, tensions in which we might be left dangerously unbalanced if either side were let go of for the sake of greater clarity or comfort. We could end up barreling down a highway with all accelerator and no brakes.

Another crucial thing to understand in navigating the Bible's diverse words on particular subjects is that while God's core character and desires never change, God is profoundly responsive to context. As anyone who has parented more than one child quickly discovers, an approach that worked well in nurturing one does not necessarily transfer to another. The loving, faithful action in one situation might look different from another in which the factors have changed. New circumstances may illuminate new aspects of a question. Love and holiness operate within distinct parameters, but they do not always exercise their mandate in exactly the same way.

This all means that when we ask what the Bible thinks about wealth, we should expect that the answer will be as complicated as money itself. Each biblical writer is addressing God's truth to different people in different situations, with different questions involved. Each book holds a bit of truth that exists in a dialectical relationship with the others. Living with wisdom and integrity might well lead to material blessing, as Proverbs and the Law suggest. But this isn't always the case. Revelation observes that in some cases, obedience to God might come at a high economic cost. Wealth is not evil, but as Jesus points out, loving it sure is. Any blessing that wealth provides must be held in productive tension with recognition of wealth's power to seduce, distract, and spiritually suffocate.

The question of foreign marriages in the Old Testament holds together two competing concerns. On the one hand, Israel's mission of blessing all the nations is frequently distorted by ethnocentrism and self-preoccupation. On the other hand, there's no faster way to become sidetracked from your distinctive values and convictions than by uniting yourself, body and soul, with someone who doesn't share your core faith allegiance. Both of these factors are real and legitimate and must somehow be accounted for.

Governments vary greatly in both form and leadership, so it probably shouldn't be a surprise that the Bible's reflections on them look slightly different in different situations. Acts suggests that open hostility need not be the default Christian response. But Revelation reminds us that idolatry lurks in the shadows of every palace, parliament, and White House and that every human kingdom, in the end, belongs to the passing darkness. The only kingdom worth entrusting with our hope is the kingdom of Christ.

When on a given subject the Bible seems to speak in several voices at once, the central question is not which voice is correct. Rather, the question is how these voices might illuminate the complexity of interlocking truths or the particularities of faithfulness in diverse contexts. Writers might well be standing on four sides of the same house, each viewing it from a different angle. The message on money most needed by an American suburbanite might be slightly different from the one needed by an orphan in a famine-stricken village. An act that in one circumstance preserves life and true faith in another situation could threaten both.

The multiplicity of voices within the Bible provides a field of possibilities on which to play out faith. The parameters of the field are set—there is such thing as a clear out-of-bounds. But within the lines, there is often a variety of possible faithful plays, every one of which might prove necessary as we consider the shape of Christ-centered obedience in an almost infinite variety of contexts.

30

YOU CAN'T HANDLE THIS
The Role of the Spirit

It's possible at this point that you might be starting to panic, thinking, "This application process feels like nuclear science! How on earth will I ever know if I'm understanding an ancient text rightly, let alone correctly applying it to my own situation?"

It's a feeling that must have been familiar to the first Christians. After all, they had the Old Testament, but its story had taken a turn in Jesus that nobody saw coming. Now they had a whole host of new questions about how knowing him changes things. As the story of Jesus spread across the world, more questions were raised every day about how the words of an ancient Jewish book and the teachings of a Jewish rabbi applied to new cultures and contexts.

The good news is that Jesus himself had seen this dilemma coming and directly addressed the anxiety it would raise. Mere hours before his death, Jesus said to his followers, "I have much more to say to you, but you can't handle it now. However, when the Spirit of Truth comes, he will guide you in all truth. He won't speak on his own, but will say whatever he hears and will proclaim to you what is to come. He will glorify me, because he will take what is mine and proclaim it to you" (John 16:12-14).

Jesus had managed to fit a whole lot into three short years with his disciples. But there were subjects they hadn't gotten to. Jesus has more to say, and they still aren't ready to hear it, and now their time together is nearly up. But that's okay. Jesus isn't in a hurry. He doesn't have to spend his final hours transcribing some grand "last lecture," cramming in the two-thirds of the syllabus they never got to because Thomas kept asking stupid questions and every story had to be explained at least three times.

The reason Jesus isn't worried is because he knows that he has backup, someone coming whom he calls "the Spirit of Truth." It's the Spirit's job to keep on speaking Jesus' mind, even after he's gone. Did you catch that? Even after his death, resurrection, and return to heaven, Jesus has a plan to keep on talking.

In John 14:25-26, Jesus offers his followers a copy of the Spirit's job description: "I have spoken these things to you while I am with you. The Companion, the Holy Spirit, whom the Father will send in my name, will teach you everything and will remind you of everything I told you." One role of the Spirit, according to Jesus, is to recall the right words at exactly the right times. When you toss your dishes in the sink for the next guy to worry about, you just might catch a whispered thought, "Jesus looked out for the interests of others, not himself" (see Philippians 2:4-5). Or when you're about to give a rude coworker a piece of your mind, you might suddenly hear a small voice calling, "Defeat evil with good" (Romans 12:21). This inconvenient voice is the Spirit, whose job it is to bring the character of Jesus home.

But Jesus goes further. He also says that the Spirit is a teacher, that the Spirit is his plan to continue conversation in years to come. This is the point at which many readers begin to get nervous. I mean, what exactly is Jesus implying? Is he suggesting the Spirit could reveal something totally new? Could the Spirit even say something that contradicts what Jesus had said earlier? Could it be like Aristotle going, "That Plato, he was real smart, but he got a few things wrong"?

On this fact Jesus is clear: the Spirit does not speak independently; the Spirit can only deliver what's taken directly from Jesus himself. Jesus was and always will be the defining expression of the Word and Will of God. God's revelation in the life, death, and resurrection of Jesus is what it is and will be forever. Unlike the rest of us mortals, Jesus will never wake up one day with writer's remorse and think, "Dang, I really wish I hadn't said that . . ."

That being said, one of the things we've learned from Jesus is that God is in intimate relationship with the world, acutely attuned to the particularity of context. God is wise, and it's the nature of wisdom to apply the right truth in the right way for the right time. Jesus guided his disciples like this while he was with them. Sometimes he said, "Whoever isn't against us is for us" (Mark 9:40). Other times he said, "Whoever isn't with me is against me" (Matthew 12:30). Jesus recognized that when he was gone, the need for such contextualized guidance wouldn't end. Circumstances would change. Christianity would move from persecuted sect to the religion of empires; populations would shift from farms to cities; norms around household roles would change; questions would arise that no one asked before—about drones, pornography, genetic modification, the relationship of faith to democratic government. New and complex situations would emerge that would require application of Jesus' truth in new and complex ways.

This was one reason why the Spirit was absolutely necessary. The Spirit bridges the gap between here and there, then and now. The Spirit teaches contextualization, how the truth about Jesus applies to an infinite variety of situations. The Spirit reveals what God is up to at any given moment and instructs Jesus' followers on what they can do to get on board.

We've seen that our task as interpreters is to read the Bible backward from Jesus, the defining revelation of God that shines clarifying light on everything before. But perhaps the even greater challenge is to read life *forward* in the light of Jesus. This is what we see the early Christians learning in Acts and the Epistles: how to read their own first-century Roman context and questions in the light of Christ. This is exactly the kind of work that the Spirit was given to lead.

A telling example of how this work of reading forward plays out is 1 Corinthians 7, in which Paul explores how marriage and singleness should be practiced among Christians—a hazardous topic if one ever existed. On the question of divorce, Paul explains that he is "passing on the Lord's command" (7:10). This is a topic Jesus had explicitly addressed in his teachings, and therefore all Paul has to do is pass along what Jesus has said: couples should stay married if at all possible.

Just a few sentences later, however, Paul takes up the question of what a new Christian convert in first-century Corinth should do if married to a nonbeliever. Here Paul's response grows more complex. He counsels that those whose spouses are willing to stay married should oblige them, but that spouses who are unwilling should be permitted a divorce.

Paul notes when he offers this counsel that "the Lord didn't say this specifically" (7:12). Jesus taught plenty of things Paul finds relevant to this situation—a high value on marriage as well as the importance of living in peace with others. Yet Paul has arrived at this particular conclusion not directly but by thoughtfully balancing principles Jesus taught and extending them in a consistent direction.

When Paul later turns to the topic of singleness, he states, "I don't have a command from the Lord . . . but I'll give you my opinion as someone you can trust because of the Lord's mercy" (7:25). On this subject Paul has neither a known statement from Jesus nor a closely related principle to extend. So he simply offers his opinion that "because of the present crisis," single people are happier staying as they are (7:26). This is a judgment call, responsive to the particular context. The calculus might well look different in another circumstance. But Paul also makes it evident he doesn't think he's simply making this stuff up on his own. "I think that I have God's Spirit too," he says (7:40). Despite Jesus having given no specific word on this situation, Paul believes he's being guided by the Spirit, who speaks from Jesus, in the present response to circumstances that have no real precedent.

We have here in one passage instructional material derived from three sources: a teaching of Jesus recalled, principles Jesus taught extended to a situation he didn't address, and a new insight derived by listening to the Spirit. All of these count, for Paul. All have weight. All these words are gifts from God to guide the community in what's right. But the care Paul takes to distinguish between the three sources implies these words must be weighed differently. A direct command from Jesus has greater weight than an extended principle; an extended principle weighs more than a Spirit-discerned opinion. Filled with the Spirit, Paul's voice is trustworthy and reliable, but only Jesus drinks from the source of pure divinity.

By the power of the Spirit, Paul is reading life forward in light of Jesus. This is what the early Christians did, carrying the teachings of Jesus forward into constantly new situations. Truth be told, the first Christians weren't always in agreement on what the Spirit was saying. They argued. They tried things out. They held councils and made speeches. They changed their minds. And slowly—not without dispute or pain or error—they began to work it out. In some cases, they discovered that not every question had a one-size-fits-all answer. Relationship to government might look slightly different in Luke's situation than in John's. Church leadership could take different forms in various times. Faithful response to the revelation of Jesus sometimes took genuinely different shapes in different communities and circumstances.

In many ways, it seems incredibly risky, this act of reading forward in light of Jesus. You might wonder, "Who are *we* to make such calls?" But the early Christians dared precisely because of what Jesus taught. All Scripture is inspired, "God-breathed" (2 Timothy 3:16 NIV); its living words are powered by God's own oxygen.

But there is something else that Jesus told them was fueled by the same power source. In John 20:22, the newly resurrected Jesus appears in a room where his disciples are hiding, breathes on them, and says, "Receive the Holy Spirit." In Genesis 2:7, human beings first come alive when God fills their lungs with God's breath. With Jesus and the giving of the Spirit, John sees that breath returning to God's people.

Creation is, in some real way, beginning all over again. All Scripture is God-breathed, and the gathered community of Jesus followers is also now filled with God's own living breath.

This is why early Christians felt comfortable using the term *inspired* broadly, to refer not only to the Bible but even occasionally to decisions of the gathered Christian community. This doesn't mean that the word of an individual or church should be given the same weight as the Bible. The words of the Bible are unique in being tested by diverse communities over thousands of years for their reliable witness to the story of faith. They are also unique in coming from people who knew Jesus best. And, as we have seen in Paul, the words and deeds of Jesus stand in a class all their own: "No one can lay any other foundation besides the one that is already laid, which is Jesus Christ" (1 Corinthians 3:11).

However, the early church believed that the God who breathed in the Bible also breathed in the Spirit-filled company of people who belong to Christ. They had not a low view of Scripture but a very high view of the Spirit's involvement in the gathered community of faith. Jesus was still present among them, still guiding, teaching, talking, even when he was no longer visible. Best we can tell, he never intended to stop. Which means that in some mysterious way, the community of Jesus in every age was actually designed and equipped for exactly this act of daring—that of listening and responding to a living God.

STORYTIME

Unwrapping Acts 3

THEY'RE ORDINARY PEOPLE, Peter and John—fishermen from a backwater village who occasionally return from the night shift with nothing in their nets but a waterlogged shoe. They'd be unremarkable, except for the one thing they've come to be known for—stepping on the back of Jesus' heels everywhere he goes.

When Jesus raises a young girl from the dead, they're present in the bedroom. When Jesus glows like bottled lightning, they stand on the mountain beside him (where "stand beside" means "cower on the ground somewhere nearby with their cloaks thrown over their heads"). When Jesus prays so hard he's sweating blood in the garden, they're right there (sleeping) next to him.

Now that Jesus has gone back to heaven, they have more time on their hands.

At three o'clock when the trumpets sound, announcing the evening sacrifice, Peter and John weave their way through the crowded streets and up to the temple to pray. As they climb the massive temple steps—210 feet wide and solid stone—four men hurry past them, each holding one corner of a makeshift stretcher. A fifth man is lumped rather awkwardly in the mat's concave center. The four men set him down on the stone at the top of the stairs, just beyond the temple walls, and then the four of them pass through the arched gates into the temple for prayer. The fifth man remains lying outside.

Even today the world is often inhospitable to those with disabilities, but the ancient world is particularly unforgiving. This man can't work. He can't run away from trouble. He can't support a family of his own. His survival depends on handouts from people who don't even have the courage to meet his eyes as they toss a few coins in his cup. According to the Law, a man in his condition is unfit to serve in the priestly class that offers sacrifices and approaches the holy place in the center of the temple where God's presence is said to dwell. His road stops here, on God's porch. The word *sacrifice* in Hebrew means "to draw near," but the closest he's getting is whatever whiffs of offerings or snatches of prayers the wind carries outside to where he and the rest of the hopeless and broken lie.

Seeing Peter and John about to pass by him, the man calls out for pity, for a small donation. This, after all, is why he comes here day after day—temple gates are prime real estate for beggars. People who show up for evening prayers are the sort who know their religious duty to give alms—or who at least might feel guilty enough stepping over a hungry body to toss some pennies his way.

At the sound of his call, Peter and John abruptly stop and look intently at him. This is the first Christian miracle—a simple act of looking. The truth is, Peter and John must have passed this man a thousand times before today. After all, he's carried here daily. He was lying on the same step a few months ago when they entered with Jesus by this same gate. But for whatever reason, on this day for the first time, Peter and John actually see him. This time they don't just see an inconvenient mass of flesh obstructing the temple door. They don't just see a tidal wave of human need waiting to wash them under. This time they look and just see him—a man whose legs are thin and spindly from lack of food and lack of use. And they think, "Maybe, with Jesus' help, we can do something for this one."

Peter says to the man, "Look at us." Here is the second Christian miracle—the man looks back. A one-directional look is staring. It is pity, charity. A two-directional look is eye contact. It's the start of a relationship.

The man is expecting to receive something. There's just one problem—Peter and John belong to a new community that has as one of its distinguishing markers a commitment to share their possessions with each other as long as any have need. By three in the afternoon, their pockets are already empty. "I have no money," Peter says, and the man's face starts to fall. "But wait . . ."

There is something Peter does possess besides his empty purse. Not many days ago, Peter and John were gathered in a room together with their friends when they heard a sound like rushing wind and saw what looked like fire falling. These turned out to be heralds announcing the arrival of a gift Jesus had promised—the Holy Spirit. The same power and presence of God that had been at work in Jesus in his earthly ministry was now given to his followers to continue what he started. Peter, filled with the Spirit, knows exactly what Jesus would do in this situation. "In the name of Jesus Christ the Nazarene," he says to the man, "rise up and walk!"

Then Peter reaches down and takes the man by the right hand. This detail might seem at first rather strangely specific. The right hand? Why not just tell us what he had for breakfast, for all the relevance it has? But the right hand, in the Old Testament, is a symbol of strength. God marched on the right to fight for people in battle. It's the right hand that God grasped when God claimed someone.

"I, the Lord your God, hold your right hand," proclaims the prophet Isaiah. "It is I who say to you, 'Do not fear, I will help you'" (Isaiah 41:13 NRSV).

In Isaiah it's God who speaks these words, but in Acts it's Peter who enacts them. Standing there in Jesus' footprints, filled with the Spirit of God, Peter takes hold of a lame man's right hand. The power of the Holy Spirit, unleashed by Jesus' name, surges through Peter's body and pours into the man. It pumps through his heart and runs down his limbs. His feet and ankles abruptly become strong, and grasping Peter's hand, he rises.

This man doesn't just walk—he comes up leaping. A grown man leaps and bounds his way straight into the temple, into the presence of God. The prophet Isaiah had once described a scene like this, in his picture of what the world would be when God's re-creative work began:

> Strengthen the weak hands,
>   and support the unsteady knees.
> Say to those who are panicking:
>   "Be strong! Don't fear!
>   Here's your God,
>   coming with vengeance;
>   with divine retribution
>   God will come to save you."
>
> Then the eyes of the blind will be opened,
>   and the ears of the deaf will be cleared.
> *Then the lame will leap like the deer,*
>   and the tongue of the speechless will sing.
> Waters will spring up in the desert,
>   and streams in the wilderness.
> The burning sand will become a pool,

and the thirsty ground, fountains of water.
The jackals' habitat, a pasture;
    grass will become reeds and rushes . . .
The Lord's ransomed ones will return and enter Zion with singing,
    with everlasting joy upon their heads.
Happiness and joy will overwhelm them;
    grief and groaning will flee away.
            (Isaiah 35:3-7, 10, emphasis mine)

Isaiah captured this man's story ahead of time. This is what salvation looks like in both of the Bible's Testaments. It looks like deserts blooming, and a choir of mutes, and the deaf dancing to the music, and a lame man leaping into the center of a temple at which he used to lie helpless outside.

* * * * *

During the first Christian sermon, recorded in Acts 2, Peter announces that anyone who calls on the name of the Lord will be saved. The name to which he refers is Jesus Christ of Nazareth, and in Acts 3 we see it happen just as Peter has said. But the remarkable thing about this story is that the lame man isn't the one who calls on this name, at least at first. Peter and John are the ones who call it on his behalf. And salvation comes running. The man rises to his feet in his newfound freedom, and the first place he goes of his own volition is straight into the temple.

Acts calls the place the lame man enters "the Beautiful Gate." The description likely constitutes a reference to the Nicanor gate on the east side of the temple, considered particularly lovely. According to Jewish tradition, the east gate of the temple was the one through which God passed (see Ezekiel 44:1-3). This gate faces the Mount of Olives, the direction from which Jesus entered

Jerusalem on a donkey on Palm Sunday. This gate was specifically associated with God's presence manifest in the anointed Messiah, and it is at this gate that the name of that Messiah, Jesus Christ of Nazareth, allows a lame man to enter fully into the presence of God.

Acts 3:11 tells us the healed man "clung" to Peter and John. The phrase isn't meant to imply that the man was feeling clingy, like a toddler just learning to walk. The word actually means something like "cleaved," a term used to describe the lasting commitment of marriage. Peter and John operate in this story as representatives of the entire Christian community. In passing through the Beautiful Gate, the gate of the Messiah, and in becoming bound to Jesus of Nazareth, this man has also been bound to them. He now cleaves to the church, the company of those whose purses are empty but who are filled with the power of God for the salvation of bodies, minds, and souls. From this day forward, for better or worse, this man has found his people.

These followers of Jesus are witnesses to Jesus' story, but they are also something more—conduits of his presence and power. They're sent out so that wherever they go, the leaping and dancing can start now. Jesus announced his ministry by quoting Isaiah:

> The Spirit of the Lord is upon me,
>> because the Lord has anointed me.
> He has sent me to preach good news to the poor,
>> to proclaim release to the prisoners
>> and recovery of sight to the blind,
>> to liberate the oppressed,
>> and to proclaim the year of the Lord's favor. (Luke 4:18-19)

This mission of Jesus unfolds wherever his followers carry out their mission as ambassadors of his salvation.

"Why do you stare at us," Peter asks the crowds, "as if we made this man walk by our own power or piety?" It's easy to read the story and wonder who is adequate for such a mission. Who among us is sufficiently holy or powerful or courageous to carry it out? But Peter says that it's not us. It's not our power or lack thereof. It's not our goodness or its absence. It's not our strength or weakness. It's not our know-how or ignorance. It's not about what the name of Peter or Pablo or John or Jenna can do. It's about doing the thing that only one name has ever been adequate for.

This is the future the Bible holds out to those who follow Jesus and are empowered by the Spirit: a chance to do what Jesus did, and maybe even more (see John 14:12-14). This is what Scripture reveals: a world raised up for leaping, one right hand at a time.

31

THE DISPUTE
A Case Study in Discernment

This business of listening to the Spirit and living forward in light of Jesus might sound challenging. Fortunately, the book of Acts offers a detailed snapshot of what such a process looked like in practice among the early Christians.

For most of Israel's history, there were a few markers that set people apart as belonging to the community of faith. If you were male, the most important such marker was circumcision. For both men and women, another key marker was dietary restrictions that treated certain foods as simply off limits ("unclean"). These practices, clearly prescribed in the Old Testament, were not just a common cultural accessory—like Oregonians wearing Birkenstocks with socks or midwesterners baptizing fruits in whipped cream and vegetables in vats of cream of chicken soup. Rather, circumcision and these dietary restrictions were seen as essential to distinguishing who did and who did not truly belong to the faithful people of God.

In Acts 10, during his usual pre-dinner prayer time, the apostle Peter sees a vision of a sheet coming down from heaven. The sheet is piled high with tasty animals, some of which were permissible for a faithful member of Israel to eat, others of which were not. Peter hears a voice saying to him, "Get up, Peter! Kill and eat!"

Peter flatly refuses to comply—and not because, as with some of us, the prospect of decapitating his own chicken has instantly transformed him into a vegan. He is a good, God-honoring Jew who would never deliberately violate an established command. While some of these animals are certainly kosher, they're mingling on the same tablecloth with those that are not and therefore must surely be tainted by association. That's when Peter hears the voice speak to him again: "Never consider unclean what God has made pure."

Peter is completely baffled as to what this could mean—although the fact that the vision repeats three times suggests that God might be trying to communicate something rather important. While Peter is still pondering what to make of what he's seen, the Spirit interrupts his musings to inform him that there are three men waiting for him downstairs and that he should go with them without questions because they've been sent by God.

Obeying the voice of the Spirit, Peter follows these men to the home of a centurion named Cornelius. Cornelius is not a Jew. He has not done the things required to be a full member of the people of faith—he isn't circumcised, and he doesn't follow the full extent of the Jewish Law. But he is a man who prays, gives generously to the poor, and seeks after Israel's God. Like Peter, he has recently had a vision. In Cornelius's vision, an angel gave him an address and told him to send for a man named Peter who was staying there.

Entering the house, Peter finds a large group of people like Cornelius gathered, and he ends up sharing with them the story of Jesus. As Peter is still talking, the Holy Spirit suddenly falls on everyone in the house. It's easy to tell when this happens, because everyone in the room suddenly starts praising God in languages they've never learned—exactly what happened to Peter and the rest of the Jewish Christians when God's Spirit was given to them in Acts 2.

This situation presents a real dilemma for Peter and the law-abiding Jews who are traveling with him. On the one hand, they've just watched God give a group of uncircumcised people the same crucial gift of God's presence (the Spirit) that God gave the circumcised ones. On the other hand, circumcision has served for thousands of years as the definitive identifying marker of who belonged to God. That's not something that anyone could, or should, easily let go.

But soon more and more non-Jews like Cornelius are coming to faith in Jesus, and a real dispute breaks out about whether these new groups of people converting to Jesus should now be required to be circumcised and follow Old Testament dietary laws. Some people, like missionaries Paul and Barnabas, who work with Gentiles every day, say the old markers are simply no longer necessary. Others believe they are absolutely vital. In Acts 15, the early Christians finally draw a group together to discern what God really wants.

Recall that Peter, Jesus' right-hand man and a leader among the disciples, has already had a dramatic vision which suggested that following the Law might not be necessary in order to be acceptable to God. But the vision of one person, even one as important as Peter, is not on its own enough to decide the matter for the church. Peter might well have heard from God, but there's a slim chance that what he thought he heard was the result of a bad night's sleep and a spoiled tuna sandwich. So the church gathers the apostles and elders—mature, trusted local leaders who are deeply committed to Jesus and know their Scriptures well—in order to try to discern where the Spirit of God is leading.

The first thing they do is tell stories. Everyone gathered in the room begins with one core, shared assumption: God isn't sitting away on some distant throne, waiting for someone else to do something; God is genuinely, personally active in the world. In the unfolding Christian drama, God is the lead actor, not just the director. Therefore, evidence of God's real activity ought to be discernable in the concrete marks it leaves. They sift through their collective experiences like miners panning for gold—searching for the glimmer of evidence about what God, through the Spirit, might be up to. Peter describes the series of visions that brought him and Cornelius together, and the dramatic conversions that resulted from their meeting. Paul and Barnabas share what they experienced on the mission field when they told the story of Jesus and saw people across the Roman Empire coming to trust in him.

Once the stories are collected, the group then turns to the Scriptures to try to figure out how these experiences together should be interpreted, where all this evidence is pointing. They bring what they believe they've observed of the Spirit's activity and hold it up to the Bible, asking how what they have seen aligns—or doesn't—with the larger story line of God's revealed character and intentions for the world. It's one thing, after all, for a plot to take an unexpected twist. It's a distinctly different experience (as I myself have twice discovered) to be reading along and find that someone has accidentally glued in pages from a different book.

James points the group to an Old Testament passage from Amos 9:11-12, which seems to suggest that God has always had a plan to draw non-Jews into Israel's faith. Reading backward, James sees hints in the biblical story—largely overlooked until now—that this influx from all nations is what God was building toward all along. While no one had expected that it would look like this, what the Spirit appears to be doing is consistent with what God has always claimed to want. The Spirit's methods seem a bit, well, unorthodox, but the ends haven't changed at all. The plot has twisted, but the community of faith is undeniably still being drawn together along the same story line.

Once they have weighed the experiential evidence of the Spirit's work and asked how it aligns with God's past revelations, the gathered leaders are finally in a position to make a judgment call. If God has been working all along to draw all people to faith, they decide that they shouldn't make this process any harder than necessary by enforcing laws that the Spirit appears to be bypassing. Therefore, circumcision and dietary observance will not be required. But non-Jews will be asked to keep four specific Jewish laws—avoiding idolatry, sexual immorality, eating meat from strangled animals, and consuming blood. Some of these instructions involve clear ethical components, but others seem to have been selected to avoid offending their fellow Jewish believers in ways that might create unnecessary obstacles to relationship.

No one "wins" this early dispute. Paul doesn't dance around the goalpost; James doesn't spike the football. The outcome is something neither side could have predicted; it challenges both in different ways. It reflects not so much a "compromise position" as a genuine discernment of faithful response to God's character, overall mission, and present activity. The decision the council writes and sends out to the churches is accompanied by a statement that "the Holy Spirit has led us to the decision" (Acts 15:28). This is exactly what Jesus had promised the Spirit would do—guide them, teach them, remind them so that they were able to recognize God's desires at each step along the way.[1]

The decision made in Acts 15 doesn't settle things once and for all. The judgment made by representatives of the church still has its detractors. But this process of discernment gives the church a direction in which to move. The reliability of the judgment will be revealed by time and practice as it becomes clear what has resulted.

In this case, with the benefit of thousands of years of hindsight, we might dare to conclude that the church discerned well. All of us today who call ourselves followers of Jesus but lack Jewish heritage are here because of this story. We are followers of Jesus precisely because of the new, global chapter in the story of faith opened up by this Acts 15 decision.

32

CONCORDANCE BUSTERS
Discerning Spirit and Scripture

The discernment process in Acts 15 includes two key steps: observation of the Spirit's present activity and reflection on how this perceived activity aligns—or doesn't—with the Bible's testimony to the character and intentions of God. Each of these steps presents its own distinct challenge: First, in the absence of an embossed card or blaring walk-up song, how do you recognize when the Spirit shows up? Second, when you want to test a so-called "Spirit sighting" against the witness of the Bible, which of the 1,189 chapters do you read?

In the story of Acts, there are two distinguishable sorts of "evidence" of the Spirit's activity that come into play. The first kind of evidence involves direct, supernatural encounter. Peter and Cornelius both have dramatic visions that move them toward each other. Peter also feels prompted in the midst of prayer to go downstairs to greet visitors he has no way of knowing are present, and he finds the situation to be exactly as the Spirit has said (Acts 10:19-21).

To be sure, there are many kinds of voices a person might hear in their head, and anyone trying to learn to distinguish

God's from the rest knows it's easy to make mistakes. But despite the possibility of mishearing, the early Christians clearly held as a foundational conviction that God continued to speak by the Spirit and was able to be heard. On Pentecost, the day on which the Spirit whom Jesus had promised finally arrived, Peter preached from the book of Joel. In Joel's time, a special class called the prophets had the job of hearing from and speaking for God. But Joel promised that a new day was coming when God's Spirit would be poured out on everyone, and that all who received the Spirit would prophesy (see Acts 2:17-18). This day, Peter announces in the very first Christian sermon, has officially begun: any follower of Jesus is equipped by the Spirit to serve as a vessel of God's words.

The early Christians took this possibility very seriously. When a trusted person, formed deeply by prayer and habits of faithful practice, believed she or he had heard a word from God, it was worth paying attention. This was especially true when, as was the case with Peter and Cornelius, that word was confirmed by more than one witness. Such private experiences were not publicly verifiable, but the outcome certainly was. After all, Cornelius would not have found Peter without having been supernaturally handed a name and address. These kinds of experiences carried real weight, could be real manifestations of God's involvement in the world.

But an individual's private experience of God, however compelling, is never sufficient on its own to bind a whole community. This is where a second form of evidence enters into the picture. This is the evidence Paul and Barnabas bring to the table in Acts 15. They've been telling Jesus' story to Gentiles on the mission field, and when they do, people aren't just listening with interest—they are reorienting their entire lives in allegiance to him.

What we see here is the single most important piece of evidence of the Spirit's activity: people being drawn to Jesus and transformed into his likeness. In his letter to the Galatians, Paul describes what he calls "the fruit of the Spirit"—love, joy peace, patience, kindness, goodness, faithfulness, gentleness, and self-control (Galatians 5:22-24). The "fruit" is not a to-do list. It's a description of what people begin to look like when the Spirit is working within them to reshape them into the image of Jesus. One fruit tree might grow from happenstance. But no one who stumbles on a field of trees laden with rows of cherries and peaches and oranges and avocados would be led to conclude that it appeared in this form by sheer coincidence. Where people are being radically and comprehensively re-formed, it's safe to conclude that the Spirit is farming.

The other primary work of the Spirit is empowering Jesus' people with what Paul calls "spiritual gifts" (1 Corinthians 12): capacities to participate in Jesus' mission of announcing a new world approaching. When Peter shares the story of Jesus at Cornelius's house, everyone starts to speak in different languages. This isn't some weird, random side effect of a spiritual high. What these people have received is the capacity to share the good news of God's work with others who haven't yet heard it. When people gain abilities they didn't previously possess that allow them to share in Jesus' mission, there's good reason to suspect the Spirit is involved.

Where we see any of these indications of the Spirit's activity, it's a sign to stop and pay attention. We might be surprised—as the first Christians clearly were—about where God is working, and how, and with whom. The story sometimes takes turns we didn't predict. If we aren't staying attuned to the Spirit, we might not only miss the juncture; we can actually become an obstacle impeding God's own movement.

But as convincing as lived experiences of the Spirit might feel, the early Christians recognized there was always a real danger that such a powerful train could pick up too much speed and jump the tracks. That is why there must also exist an "evaluation system" that sets off warning bells if the turns are being taken too quickly or if the train is on the verge of flying off the course. This is where the Bible comes in. Every experience of the Spirit had to be rigorously tested to ensure it maintained alignment with the past revelation of God, manifest in the history of Israel and above all made known in the witness of Jesus Christ.

When James and his fellow leaders turn to the Bible, they identify Amos 9 as the biblical passage that speaks the word from God most relevant to their current circumstances. This might strike us as a rather strange textual selection. After all, the topic on the table is whether non-Jews must be circumcised to belong to the people of faith, and Amos 9 doesn't mention circumcision at all. If you wanted to know what God thinks about circumcision, it seems that the most obvious place to look would be Genesis 17, the passage in which the practice is first instituted. In this passage, God establishes a covenant with Abraham that includes one central sign: "Circumcise every male," including "those who are not your own children" (Genesis 17:10, 12)—in other words, anyone joining the family from the outside.

But James and the early Christians are reading their Bibles in a radically new fashion. They are reading Scripture backward, in light of Jesus, who has thoroughly disrupted all they'd once thought they understood. Jesus has started a new covenant, rearranged the story's pieces, and illuminated a larger plotline threading its way through the biblical text—the story of a God seeking to reconcile the whole world to God's self. This revelation changes everything, interpretively speaking. It's no longer enough to simply ask, "What did God say to Abraham about circumcision?" Now they must ask, "What has God revealed in Jesus, and in the whole of the Scriptures Jesus illuminates, that God is trying to accomplish in the world?"

For these early Christian interpreters, it is not Genesis alone or Amos alone that speaks definitively but Genesis and Amos and all the books together, now read in light of Jesus. This principle of reading backward in light of Jesus means that knowing what God thinks about a given question requires more than a simple concordance search of topical keywords. It requires understanding the whole story, how the pieces fit together, how they all realign in relationship to Jesus. Biblical action in the new Christian reality is not any activity that can find a verse somewhere to defend itself. Biblical action is activity that fully aligns itself with the character and mission of God revealed in Jesus. What's defining for Christians is not any single verse or passage on its own (such as Genesis 17) but the entire authoritative story of Jesus within which every individual passage speaks. To the question of which piece of the Bible we must consider in order to know God's will in a given situation, our answer must always be, in some sense, "All of it!"

Of course, when James and the early Christians undertake this process of discerning the Spirit in conversation with Scripture, they possess only the Old Testament. They are doing all their reading backward, in light of the interpretive revolution that is Jesus himself. However, when we discern our own Bibles today, we have an additional set of books to consider—the New Testament—in which followers of Jesus practice not just reading the Old Testament backward but also reading their own lives and situations forward, in light of what they've learned from Jesus. When we come to these books to discern what the Spirit may be up to in our own time, there is one key word to keep in mind: context.

We will never again have another event like the arrival of Jesus that totally upends and reconfigures the entire biblical story line. The one definitive, authoritative disruption has already occurred. It is also true, however, that the Spirit continues to apply God's defining revelation in Jesus to diverse cultures, communities, and contexts. When we read the New Testament, we are seeing leaders applying the truth of Jesus, under the Spirit's guidance, to particular situations in their own worlds, each with its own nuanced details and stakes.

This means that when we come to these New Testament texts to discern the Spirit's movement in our own place and time, we must read *wide* as well as *deep*. It is important to hold in mind both the larger revelation of Jesus in which any particular instructions are grounded and the situational specifics with which this revelation interacts to evoke this particular response. When we discern, we consider how our own situation may be similar to or different from those pictured by the text. The stronger the similarities, the greater our expectation should be of continuity between the Spirit's actions in these texts and in our own time. Where there are vital situational differences, we may find the Spirit bringing to bear the mission of Jesus using slightly different approaches but always with the same larger commitment to love, holiness, trust, and salvation. The Spirit has been known to move in surprising ways. But the destination, the mission, the end goal always remains the same: Jesus, his lordship, full commitment to calling all people into participation in God's beautifully remade world. The Spirit's creative activity never wavers from this trajectory or from full submission to Jesus' defining revelation.

This kind of discernment is risky business. It is not the sort of act that can be performed by computer searches or algorithms. It requires Spirit-filled people, actively listening for God, seeking insight into how Jesus' mission can be faithfully executed in every time and place. It must be undertaken with care, with a humble recognition of our own capacities for self-deception, self-justification, and selective listening. But this is also exactly the risk Jesus invited his followers to take—the risk of being awake to living Word and living Spirit walking in step together. The Bible speaks the foundational word of who God is and where the story is headed. The Spirit's work is to draw the pieces together so that the vision, the mission, and the truth can flourish in every circumstance.[1]

Of this we can be sure: when the pieces are properly aligned under the guidance of the Spirit, they always come out looking like Jesus Christ.

33

SEEING BLUE AND GREEN
The Role of Community

Learning to dissect a frog is different from learning to play the violin. (Thank you, Captain Obvious.) With the frog, if you follow the diagram in making the incisions, you have a decent shot at identifying the organs on the first attempt with a high level of accuracy. With the violin, as many parents have discovered to their everlasting regret, there's no diagram on earth that can make all the sounds come out right on even the hundredth try. Succeeding here requires learning to feel instinctually when your fingers are in the right spot, developing an ear able to pick up the slightest flatness in the note.

It has probably become obvious by now that the Bible is less like the frog and more like the violin. To learn to play—to live—beautifully, in concert with God, requires more than a step-by-step dissection guide. Biblical application is an art, and as such it involves an inevitable aspect of personal judgment. This is one reason that, when the early Christians wanted to know God's desires on a difficult matter, they drew together a gathering of people to discern it.

There is no question that an individual can be guided by the Spirit. Paul is converted to Christianity after hearing a voice that those beside him could not, at least not as he did (Acts 22:9). In Acts 21:11, a man named Agabus receives a message from the Spirit that Paul will be arrested if he travels to Jerusalem. Events unfold exactly as he describes. A central gift Jesus promised all who would follow him was the capacity to be in direct communication with God, and in the Bible we see this happen time and time again—ordinary people hear from God.

However, there's another reality that most people listening for God discover sooner or later—all of us are far more fallible than we like to think. Our past experiences, personality, natural inclinations, race, gender, culture, class, and historical context all influence the ways we read, think, and see the world. Each of us comes to the biblical text with a particular angle of vision that predisposes us to some insights and blocks us from others. I have friends in North America who assume the Bible's stories of people being healed as metaphoric; I have a friend in another part of the world who spends an entire day each week praying over sick people who have walked all night to meet him. What he has seen with his own eyes causes him to hear these biblical stories quite differently.

Some languages lack terms to distinguish between the colors blue and green. In recent studies, scientists have demonstrated that the terms available to a culture can actually affect the color differentiation its people are able to perceive. Trying to discern the Bible and Spirit alone leaves us profoundly vulnerable to our own blind spots, prone to confirmation bias and to seeing only that which we already possess terms to categorize.

"Whatever you fasten on earth will be fastened in heaven," Jesus says in Matthew 18:18. "And whatever you loosen on earth will be loosened in heaven." This might sound like a lot of cryptic talk from life BZ (Before Zipper), but in Jesus' day the language of "fastening" and "loosening" was associated with interpretation of the Scriptures. Rabbis had authority to "bind and loose" application of biblical texts for those who followed them—in other words, the authority to say what could and could not be done.[1] This authority of application Jesus explicitly ascribes to the church: the assembly of those committed to following him.

Of course, the obvious question this raises is, Which church? Which community of people has authority to say what Scripture means and what should be done about it? This has been a dilemma for thousands of years, with different bodies of people making competing claims to speak for God. The Bible, sadly, does not answer this question by saying, "You, in this community here, totally get God, unlike that church down the block that is full of total loons."

Acts does, however, suggest a couple of characteristics of a community that is functioning in its work of binding and loosing with genuine spiritual authority. The first thing to note about the people gathered in the room in Acts 15 is that they are relatively diverse (at least by standards of first-century Palestine), coming in with different concerns and predispositions. Paul, a missionary to the Gentiles, is an infamous pragmatist, willing to part ways with ancient traditions in a heartbeat if it helps the good news about Jesus break through cultural barriers. James, leader of the Jewish church in Jerusalem, is conservative in the technical sense of the word—he values the Law, history, and tradition. Also present is Peter, leader among the twelve disciples, who might be generously called a moderate—or, as Paul might less graciously put it, be prone to situational flip-floppery (see Galatians 2:11-14).

Truth be told, in discerning the Bible in a gathering of people who share our culture, life experience, social location, and general worldview, the risk—much like with reading individually—is that our biases and assumptions go unchallenged. I was quite dismissive of the Bible's cursing psalms until I read them in Gulu, Uganda, after meeting with women who were kidnapped by soldiers as young girls and forced to be child brides. It turns out I simply didn't have the kind of experience that allowed me to make sense of these psalms. But these women did. Whoever we are and whatever our location, discerning the Bible well requires listening in the presence of others whose experiences and assumptions are different from our own.

It's worth noting that many books in the New Testament are written for communities who are struggling simply to keep food on the table day by day and who in many cases are suffering additional social and economic hardships because of their Christian commitment. Those in our own time who share these sorts of formative experiences in common with the Bible's first writers and readers may be particularly well positioned to offer vital insights on the text—insights those of us who live in more privileged settings might overlook. When we consider the voices gathered around the interpretive table, these may be especially valuable to attend to.

As valuable as diversity is, however, it cannot stand on its own. For a community to function meaningfully *as* a community, rather than just be a gathering of random individuals, it requires some kind of center, some common element or shared purpose. The church has a single, unshakable center:

allegiance to the resurrected Jesus and obedience to his Way. This is the unifying core that gives diversity its meaning. In the book of Revelation's vision of heaven, people are gathered from every tribe, tongue, and nation, but they fall down in one common act of worship before the throne of God.

When the church in Acts 15 wanted to know what God was saying, they didn't call a vote of anyone who could hold a ballot. Democracy and discernment are not at all the same thing. As one of my former professors liked to point out, consensus killed Jesus.[2] The church in Acts 15 was seeking the will of God, not the will of the majority; the voice of God, not the voice of whoever shouted loudest. The people who gathered in discernment were committed to the faith, trusted for their judgment and their spiritual grounding.

The ability to distinguish the Spirit's voice is certainly not exclusively (or even reliably) the property of religious professionals or people with degrees. But it's also not a skill developed overnight. It is a capacity cultivated through a consistent set of practices that shapes us into individuals and communities who are equipped to listen well.

Unlike other skills like, say, juggling knives or speaking Portuguese, this is a skill in which character matters. A community that is equipped to hear God on the difficult questions is one already deeply invested in a process of being transformed into the character of Christ. It must be experienced enough in the practice of repentance to have developed humility, an ability to recognize its own inner darkness and capacity for error. It must have spent enough time in the Bible not just to know how to navigate the concordance but to have developed a holistic new imagination for the world. It must have spent enough time in prayer to be practiced in picking God's still, small voice out of all the chaos. It must be formed deeply enough by worship to have developed a posture of submission. It must have walked the Jesus Way far enough to be practiced in prioritizing the interests of others, even at personal cost.

There is no shortcut to the formational work these practices cultivate. Waiting until crisis strikes to consider them is like waiting to learn medicine until your hand is wrapped around someone's spleen. By then, the odds are high it's already too late to develop the necessary dexterity. The community that is formed to hear God clearly is not just any random collection of people but a collection of people who are shaped by habits of obedience, trust, and careful listening. They are people who have claimed their allegiance to Jesus over their own agenda and have significant practice separating the two.

For some, all this talk about authority and community might be concerning. After all, those who consider themselves Protestant Christians trace their origins back to a time when the church had grown deeply corrupt. Others have personally experienced the pain of a community gone wrong, which claimed to speak for Christ while living out of alignment with his character.

Unfortunately, there is no foolproof solution for escaping human error. Interpreting and applying the Bible requires real human involvement—there is no other way. And where humans are involved in a task, whether individually or collectively, mistakes are inevitable. Our best hope is to listen together in full knowledge of the risks. To humbly help each other discover our undisclosed blind spots. To listen together across different frequencies. To practice reading not only through our own eyes but through the eyes of our neighbors.[3]

When we do this, even in halting, broken form, we have a fighting chance of spotting God arrayed in shades of blue and green we never would have had the language to see on our own.

34

FROZEN GODS
Holding Convictions

There's just one problem with reading the Bible in a community of others, especially those who are very different from you. Sometimes all those other people are flat-out wrong.

Just kidding. But really: sometimes after a rigorous process of watching for the Spirit, interpreting the historical context, and applying the Bible's whole narrative arc, you still may not all agree on the outcome. This can happen even when all parties involved are deeply committed, Christ-formed people who sincerely want to know what God desires.

Seemingly against all odds, the Jerusalem Christians gathered in Acts 15 who began the conversation with diverse views appear to end up in near-miraculous agreement about what the Spirit is leading them to do. Not every such story ends so smoothly. Truth be told, even after the seemingly Spirit-led decision about the relationship of Gentiles to the Jewish Law by the group that came to be known as the Jerusalem Council, plenty of other Christians in the early church passionately disputed the group's conclusions. They continued for years to drive around the Mediterranean world flashing "No Snip, No Membership" bumper stickers.

Even where a clear consensus emerges from a process of biblical discernment, unanimity is rare. Almost always there is at least a minority of dissenters who have put the pieces together differently. Perhaps just as important as learning to faithfully discern is learning how to faithfully disagree on our conclusions. The first step in disagreeing well is considering how we hold our own hard-sought convictions about the Bible.

When the Jerusalem Council sends out the press release announcing their decision about the Gentiles, they open with a deceptively simple statement: "It seemed good to the Holy Spirit and to us" (Acts 15:28 NIV). There's more going on here than first appears. The Old Testament prophets frequently punctuated their pronouncements with the declaration "This is what the Lord says." This prophetic assertion has a certain absoluteness about it that is conspicuously missing from the decision ("It seemed good . . .") made by the Jerusalem Council.

The Christians in Acts gather evidence of the Spirit's activity, they study their Scriptures, and in the end, they make a judgment about what they think God is doing and how they are being led to participate. They feel a genuine sense of divine guidance throughout the entire process, and they go public with the conclusion of their discernment with a sense of joy and confidence that their decision will allow the church collectively to move forward in its Jesus-centered mission.

But even as they go all in on obedience to what they've discerned are God's desires, they also appear to hold their conviction with a critical strand of humility. They believe they've read the Scriptures and the Spirit's movement well, but they recognize the possibility, however small, that they could have connected the pieces incorrectly. So they move forward in applying their judgment not with a public declaration that they've established "God's final word on this matter" but with a statement that they've discerned a course of action that they believe reflects the Spirit's leading. Then they open this weighty judgment to the testing of time and experience.

The often-overlooked final step in the process of discernment is this test of time: allowing the opportunity to see how a particular judgment plays out in practice. In Deuteronomy, God instructed the people of Israel that if they wanted to know whether a prophet was actually representing God, there was one way to find out: they should give it time and see if what the prophet predicted actually happened (Deuteronomy 18:21-22). There was no shortcut, no hidden "true prophet" birthmark, no trial by fire. You couldn't verify the truth saturation of a particular prophet by dunking him in water and then checking to see if he turned blue. The validity of the prophet's hearing is revealed by the long-term result.

There was a point in the life of the early church when a decision about Gentile circumcision could no longer be delayed without seriously imperiling the mission and cohesion of the community. With their eyes on the Spirit and their Scriptures in their hands, they therefore made a judgment. But only time could tell whether their application of Amos 9, in relinquishing the necessity of Gentile circumcision, was in fact a correct representation of God's intent.

Time is powerful for several reasons. First, the Bible's own story suggests that the world has a real order and design. Some things lead to life; others to death. In the short term, it is often hard to tell which is which, but these things tend to reveal themselves by their effects over time. Jumping off the roof while holding the corners of a bedsheet might seem like an inspired idea. But sooner or later the principles of gravity make themselves known. Reality has a definitive shape we cannot alter or defy for long without experiencing the consequences.

We also have been given a Spirit who functions in the world as a genuine actor. The Spirit's real presence and independent activity mean we aren't just free to make things up. There's a living God around to actually contradict us. An individual can go astray for a time, and so can a whole community or even a whole stream of the church. But sooner or later that which is hollow exposes itself. A Jetta dressed up like the Batmobile might fool us for a while, at least from a distance, but the missing power under the hood can't be faked when the pressure is on.

The relevant indicators over time are virtually identical to those we look to in searching for initial evidence of the Spirit's activity: Has this decision led to greater allegiance to Jesus? Is it moving those affected by it toward growth in the character of Christ? Are there signs of the Spirit's fruit and spiritual gifts emerging? These things serve as possible confirmatory evidence that the hypothesis we formed about the direction of the Spirit's movement was, in fact, correct. This analysis of long-term impact is crucial, because on occasion our discernment might skew to favor short-term benefits without accurate perception of the lifetime costs.

In some cases, including many decisions in our personal lives, a few months may be enough to begin to see the trajectory of our discernment. Did the decision we made lead to greater love, loyalty, and growth in Christ in us and the people around us? If so, there's a high chance we heard well.

In other cases, such as major controversies that divide large segments of the church, it may take generations to perceive the scope of relevant results. In general, the larger the question, the more time it takes to confirm whether we've seen clearly. Discernment requires patience far beyond our normal custom, an ability to live boldly and with conviction but also with some level of tentativeness, knowing that all the pertinent information is not yet in our hands.

Over the long run, the quality more determinative than any other of how far we will grow in the wisdom of Christ is our capacity for changing direction. Our general level of "rightness" is far less important than our responsiveness to correction. God is gracious and patient and doesn't abandon us to error but keeps on guiding us toward truth. Sometimes this process of revelation takes longer than others to unfold. There is never any shame in turning around. The only shame is in continuing down a road while stepping over accumulating evidence that the path is wrong. The need for regular repentance (that is, turning) is not a sign that we have failed in our spiritual journey but that we are learning, growing, actively being shaped by ongoing engagement with God.

People often ask when we can "close the book" on the process of discernment, declare that we are done, that we know for sure what the Bible says and means on a given question. It turns out that the uncomfortable answer is never. We can, like the church in Acts, feel sure enough in our sense of leading to move forward boldly in obedience. The more time tests the judgment and verifies its fruit, the more confident we can grow that we have listened well. But there are two crucial factors that keep discernment always open, even as our confidence increases. The first is a fact of human nature—the humbling recognition that fallibility is an incurable condition. The second is a fact about the nature of God.

While God's character and mission revealed in Jesus never change, the God revealed in the Bible remains profoundly and intimately relational. As circumstances and contexts and human choices change over time, so does God's response to them. This means that while some questions possess once-for-all-time answers, others may arise that lend themselves to many diverse, faithful applications. The gospel call may sound quite different if we find ourselves in a position to sing it in a first-century field, a tent, a subway, a concert hall, the shower. It may sound different if played by a lute or an organ or an electric guitar. But it remains the same song always, in every new arrangement. This is how it is with God: one melody in many variations, one character and many contexts in which to exercise it. The key is to sing our song boldly according to the arrangement we believe has been given to us—but to always be open to the prospect of a Spirit-produced remix.

Therefore, while we would like to be able to settle things, wrap them up, draw our final conclusions, feel the pleasant emotional release that comes with certainty, the truth is that discernment is never done. This is the case both because we never mature past capacity for error and because different times may call for different responses. Anyone who is finished with discernment is finished with the living God. Those who close the process of discernment end up embalming God into the form of what the Bible calls "an idol." An idol is not necessarily a false image of God, although it may certainly be that. It can also reflect a true image, a true word, a true idea that is frozen, absolutized, made to be everything.

The God of the Bible refuses to be limited this way. God insists on being honored as free and responsive, and the only way to honor such a God is to remain constantly alert. Our job is not to have a final answer to every question but to stay awake at all times to the movement of the Spirit, whose job it is to teach us to sing the good news of Jesus in the distinctive tongue of every tribe.

35

THE GOOD FIGHT
How to Disagree Well

Okay, let's finally get down to it, the million-dollar question of biblical interpretation: What do we owe to other followers of Jesus with whom we vehemently disagree? This question takes us into complex territory in which the answer may depend very much on the context of the query.

We live in a time when divisions between followers of Jesus seem deep and intractable. Some of the issues dividing Christians are minor interpretive matters, while others cut to the very heart of the good news about Jesus and how we understand the Bible to function. It would be a disservice both to the sacred Story and to the consciences involved to pretend such differences do not matter. This is not a book about the church. But it may be worth observing that for a community of Christ followers to move forward into its mission with passion and integrity, there might be times when we must acknowledge we are not feeling led by Spirit and Scripture in the same direction and must part ways in order to faithfully move forward into our sense of our God-given calling. This can happen both to individuals within specific churches and to churches as they relate to each other across wider systems.

This is not the place to dig into the specifics of when and how such decisions should be made. Yet in a book on biblical interpretation, it is important to consider briefly how people who share a core allegiance to Jesus as risen Lord are called to treat each other across interpretive differences, regardless of whether they find themselves able to move forward together in formal cooperative mission. This is a topic Paul touches on in Romans 14–15, in perhaps one of the most revolutionary passages in the New Testament Letters.

The Christians in Rome at this time are divided over several matters. One is whether it's okay to eat meat sold in the market—which may not have been slaughtered according to kosher law and almost certainly was offered on a pagan altar before making it to the shelf. Another is whether it's necessary to observe Jewish festival days.

Now, these are both issues on which Paul himself has a clearly established position. If you've read any of Paul's letters, you've probably discovered that Paul tends to wear his opinions with all the subtlety of a 1980s tracksuit. But before he says a word on his thoughts about the actual matters in question, Paul appeals to the Romans for Jesus' sake to stop judging and looking down on one another. He goes on to write: "Someone who thinks that a day is sacred, thinks that way for the Lord. Those who eat, eat for the Lord, because they thank God. And those who don't eat, don't eat for the Lord, and they thank the Lord too. We don't live for ourselves and we don't die for ourselves. If we live, we live for the Lord, and if we die, we die for the Lord. Therefore, whether we live or die, we belong to God" (Romans 14:6-8).

Paul reminds the Romans that the most pertinent fact about any of them is their Christ-ward orientation. Whatever they are doing, they are doing not to please themselves but out of sincere desire to honor and obey the One to whom they've promised their total allegiance.

In Paul's view, it's simply not enough to be right. Composting might be good for the planet, but if I'm doing it primarily because of the satisfying sense of superiority over others that it gives me, or because I'm trying to impress the attractive hipster next door, it's not actually virtue I'm practicing. It's fully possible to take a right position in pursuit of some agenda other than pleasing Christ. And for Paul, there is only one goal worth talking about—absolute allegiance to the Lord Jesus Christ. Action that stems from any other motive than "for the Lord" is fundamentally flawed, because it forms the actor away from the submission to Christ that was the point all along.

In making this statement, Paul cleverly achieves two things at once. First, he gives the Romans a new criterion by which to measure their own behavior: not "Am I right?" but "Am I living and dying on this hill not to prove a point or defend something that I want, but solely for Jesus' sake?" The difficulty of reliably assessing even our own motives with complete certainty invites a necessary humility about our qualifications to assess the motives of others. God is the only one, Paul believes, in a position to accurately judge that which matters most: not just what we are doing but why.

The second thing Paul's statement does for the Romans is to suggest that when they look at each other, instead of seeing only their present disagreement, they might focus first on what they share: their common allegiance to Christ and their mutual accountability to him. Large and long-term disagreements have an unfortunate side effect of tunnel vision, leaving parties blind to the convictions they share. This is always more obvious to those outside the conflict, such as those who listen to Christians argue about communion wine versus communion grape juice going, "Wait, wait, wait—y'all think that those tiny glasses contain a shot of *Jesus*?!"

As emotions rise in an extended process of discernment, it is also not uncommon in Christian history for both parties to react to each other like repelling magnets, pushing each other further and further out to less helpful extremes. One way of countering this destructive repellent effect is to regularly affirm the areas of significant agreement. This helps keep the community living from its center point rather than the tenth ring out.

Perhaps Paul's most surprising statement about living with interpretive disagreement is his suggestion that to pressure others to do the right thing when it means acting against their conscience or in opposition to their sense of the Spirit's leading might actually cause them to do wrong. Paul writes, "I know and I'm convinced in the Lord Jesus that nothing is wrong to eat in itself. But if someone thinks something is wrong to eat, it becomes wrong for that person" (Romans 14:14). This ties to Paul's larger conviction that what counts is not simply the "objective" nature of the action but the reason for it. The most important defining aspect of any action is how it is orienting the actor in relation to Christ. "The right thing" may still be wrong if it represents a choice to bow to social pressure over one's inner conviction of what obedience to Christ requires. "Everything that isn't based on faith is sin," Paul says (Romans 14:23).

As much as we might wish to, we cannot forcibly speed along someone else's growth in understanding, and Paul cautions the Romans against the significant damage that can be done when we try. Stretching someone's faith too far too fast can cause it to snap, like an overextended rubber band. Faith cannot and should not be coerced, and there must be some room within the company of Jesus followers for real difference in judgments and growth stages to be expressed without calling into question the core shared allegiance that moves both parties.

Paul implies that the desire to be pleasing to God is itself pleasing to God. The most defining thing about a person may not be their correctness on the particular issue in dispute but whether their actions stem from a genuine desire to be obedient. This idea has never been a popular one. When someone is wrong, we'd really like them to know they're wrong. If we're honest, we might even secretly wish that God would thump them over the head a few times—preferably with their own Bible—until they see the light (or at least a few stars). The patience of God—upon which we ourselves so deeply rely to cover our own faults, mistakes, and blind spots, whether we realize it or not—can be the most maddening thing in the world when we see it directed toward someone with whom we profoundly disagree.

But God has never been a purist, restricting association to those who get it right. If that were God's character, the story of the Bible would have been over before it began. God's patience and tolerance for the long, painful process of learning are at the heart of the gospel's scandal. Everyone will, at times, misjudge their step. The best we can do is seek to fall forward, fall in God's direction, fall toward the intention of obedience—and judge our neighbors with charity as they also seek to stumble and fall toward Christ.

This particular knowledge—that we are all falling somewhere—suggests why it's especially important in times of disagreement to ask what we might learn from the other party's concerns. If large sections of the committed community of Christ, after a long process of discernment, continue to disagree, chances are extremely high that both sides have seen something worth attending to. Even if we continue to disagree with others on the ultimate conclusion, it is worth asking if our opponents might be calling our attention to an important aspect of the question that we could otherwise overlook. Instead of immediately seeking to close out the voice of dissent, we may be best served by stopping to ask where our eyes need to be open for our own potential for error. More than a few Jesus followers have become so busy avoiding the ditch on one side of the road—the ditch where their opponents seem so appallingly stuck—that they topple backward into the ditch they never noticed gaping on the other side.

The Jewish people have had within their own interpretive tradition a long-established practice of preserving the minority view when there has been significant disagreement. The reasoning is that even if one view wins the day, there might be a time and place in history when the minority view could be valuable, could provide the crucial thread of insight a future generation might need.[1] Christians might receive from Judaism a helpful reminder that it's impossible to always foresee what ways the future community could be challenged, what new angles of vision a future context may require.

Perhaps Paul's most important instruction to the Romans facing disagreement is that they consider what they could do to nurture the work of God in the people with whom they disagree. Paul writes in Romans, "Each of us should please our neighbors for their good in order to build them up. Christ didn't please himself, but, as it is written, 'The insults of those who insulted you fell on me'. . . . May the God of endurance and encouragement give you the same attitude toward each other, similar to Christ Jesus' attitude" (Romans 15:2-3, 5).

Paul makes clear that the kind of "building up" he has in mind is not berating the other party into agreement on the question in dispute. There's a kind of hammering that destroys rather than builds anything constructive. Rather, Paul reminds them that God's kingdom is about "righteousness, peace, and joy in the Holy Spirit" (Romans 14:17). The real question, according to Paul, is how those who disagree can continue to support the work God is doing in each other, how—disagreement aside—we can help others flourish in faith, hope, and charity and in their core allegiance to Christ.

However boldly we hold and practice our own convictions, Paul asserts strongly that nothing gives us the right to "destroy someone for whom Christ died" (Romans 14:15). In all circumstances, our treatment of each other is meant to reflect the priceless worth Christ has ascribed to us all by purchasing us with his life. No one wins when we dehumanize or destroy each other in disputes that spring from mutual desire for faithfulness. Where we cut each other down, Christ's kingdom loses on two sides.[2]

The challenge in biblical disagreement is to learn to trust the breadth of grace promised to us in our own core narrative —the atoning death of Jesus, sufficient for all sins. The church has been wrong about significant things in every age, and this is sure to be true in ours as well. We can't be sure right now which things, exactly, we are currently wrong about, but we are no exception to history. But as Paul reassuringly reminds us, in the final accounting, God is able to make us stand, and God is able to make our neighbors stand too (Romans 14:4). Salvation doesn't hinge on any of us getting everything right. The grace of Christ is big enough to cover us and those with whom we disagree. Resting in this assurance, we are all free to keep on reading, listening, and falling forward toward greater understanding and greater faithfulness.

STORYTIME

Unwrapping the Book of Job

THERE ONCE WAS a man named Job. Job was a distinguished businessman of a certain age with a glint of silver in his hair and a sparkle of humor in his eyes. He'd achieved his success in the old-fashioned way, through hard work, high moral standards, and unfailing fairness to everyone. His employees were devoted to him, and community leaders frequently stopped by to seek his advice.

Job had raised ten children who, against all odds, respected him and actually liked one another. He and his wife of thirty-five years looked forward to retirement, when they hoped to travel together and spend more time with their grandkids.

Every morning of his adult life, Job rose while it was dark and went out to walk with God. He strolled across the quiet fields, praying by name for his children, his neighbors, even his enemies. Then he climbed the small hill on the edge of town and sat in God's presence in companionable silence, watching the sun rise. When the light fully dawned, he descended and went home to family breakfast, humming a song of praise.

But one morning Job returned home from his daily prayers to find his wife weeping at the gates. While he was gone, a gang of teenage thieves had ransacked the house, smashing anything they couldn't carry. As he embraced his wife, Job caught a sudden whiff of smoke in the air and looked up to see a neighbor running down the road, shouting his name. It appeared a random lightning bolt had struck from nowhere and burned Job's factory to the ground. At that exact moment, Job's business manager showed up to break the news that their accountant had embezzled the pension fund, leaving them and their employees with nothing.

Before Job could respond, his best friend appeared, and the gathered group fell silent. Through his tears, he choked out that all ten of Job's children had been gathered for brunch when a tornado swept through, collapsing the house and killing them all. The day after the mass funeral, Job woke up in agonizing pain and received the diagnosis from the doctor: cancer, stage IV. As he lay on his bed, back rigid with pain, Job's wife sobbed hysterically, "Just curse God, and maybe he'll smite us both and put us out of our misery."

When Job's closest friends, Eli, Bill, and Zophie, heard the news and came to find him the next afternoon, he was in the garden staring blindly into space. His face was so swollen and twisted with grief that they barely recognized him. Seven full days they sat in silence together. On the eighth day, just after dawn, the silence was broken when Job started to speak: "May the day I was born be cursed forever. May a good thing never again happen on this day of the year. Why didn't I die in my mother's womb? Why didn't the nurse leave me to starve on the hospital floor? Then at least now I'd be at peace. Why, oh why, would God create someone just to torture them mercilessly?"

Job's friends cannot bear his utter despair. They can't bear to hear such terrible words from the man who taught them faith. Therefore, they grope for some helpful words, some answer or explanation that can keep the world from spinning into utter chaos.

"Job, let's think about this," Eli begins tentatively. "Don't you believe that God is just? And doesn't justice mean the wicked are punished and the righteous blessed? So then doesn't that imply that where there's terrible suffering . . . sin must be present somewhere?"

"That's right," Zophie chimes in. "Just confess whatever you've done wrong and tell God you're sorry, and God will forgive you and things will turn around."

Seeing that Job isn't biting, Bill takes a different tack. "I know it's hard to see right now," he says, "but God's discipline refines us. Don't we all have flaws, however small? Don't we all need a little polishing? None of us is a finished work, right? The good thing about suffering is that it builds character. In the end, this experience will make you even better and stronger than you already are."

At just that moment, Job's pastor, Lee, approaches—a young man fresh from seminary. He takes a deep breath and begins, "Listen, Job. I know you're hurting, but your problem is, you're making this too much about you. You'd have a better perspective if you took your eyes off yourself for a moment and spent some time meditating on the omnipotence of God."

"And in any case," Lee says, moving on to his second point, "on the other side of this, once you've experienced restoration, you'll look back on this day and recognize that your pain has served a purpose. If you hadn't suffered, you wouldn't have experienced the grace of God in putting things back together. You'll see. In the end, all things work together for good for those who love the Lord, you know."

They are reasonable arguments, even biblical ones. But Job is profoundly unmoved. "Do you think I don't know all the same things you do?" he asks with a piercing glare. "Haven't I heard all those explanations a thousand times? But can't you see that your Sunday school answers don't apply to this case? There's no explanation or promise you can make that will bear the weight of this tragedy."

"Never mind your answers," Job continues. "It's not you all I want to talk to anyway. I want an audience with God, and I'll be heard or die trying. Do you hear that, God?! Do you hear me?! What have I done that's so terrible, so wrong, that you would treat me this way? Why do you hide from me? Why do you torture me? Why do you treat me as an enemy? Or is that really what we are?"

* * * * *

The book of Job is beautiful in the same way a tornado or hurricane is beautiful. It is terrible yet transfixing, stunning and stupefying. This story blots out the sun. It uproots answers one by one and flings them aside. It demolishes towering certitudes. It shreds bumper-sticker promises and pious platitudes. It levels the land-scape of faith and leaves us standing in the wreckage.

The beginning of Job's story shows us the world as we want it to be. It's the world of our movies, where heroes prosper and villains languish. It's a world where karma functions—or, in biblical terms, where people reap what they sow. It's the world of the psalmist who assures us he's never seen the righteous forsaken or their children begging for bread. It's the world of the proverbs that insist that those with integrity walk securely and the honest reap a profit. It's a world where the generous and God-fearing live in peace, enjoying the fruit of their faithfulness.

But Job's subsequent suffering stands in the Bible as a counter-witness to all these other truths. It testifies to an experience largely unacknowledged by both cultural and religious authorities: the re-ality of genuine, unthinkable tragedy. The twenty thousand children who starve to death each day. The ride home on the bus that ends in rape. Mortar shells hitting schools and hospitals. Aid workers massacred by gangs. Tsunamis wiping villages off the map. Young mothers with cancer. Car accidents on the way to church. Lives stillborn. Dementia gradually stealing personality.

If the story of Job teaches one thing, it's this: in human suffering, there is a point at which all answers fail. Every comfort is a wound. Every explanation is a crime. Every truth itself is a lie. There's a point at which all that's left is a shattering silence and a shout of rage at a starless sky.

But then what? Is this the end of faith? Is this the moment we're finally forced to admit that God is either myth or monster? Or is there another possibility?

There once was a man whose name was Jesus. A man he was, yet so much more—all of divine perfection that could fit in human flesh. He was a gifted teacher. He loved children. He always saw the one in the crowd everyone else had missed. He stood up to bullies on behalf of the weak. He treated his enemies with kindness. He asked nothing for himself and everything for the poor. He touched the sick whom others cringed to look at. He was so intimate with God that whenever he spoke, God's own voice echoed through him.

And what did all this virtue win him? Betrayal by a friend. Denial by one of those he loved most. Abandonment in his hour of deepest need. Lies that led to a false conviction. Public mockery. Physical agony. Terrible, premature death. Darkness falls on the cross like a shroud.

After hours of tormented silence, Jesus finally finds his voice. And all he has left with his final breath is to scream at the empty sky, "Eloi, Eloi, lama sabachthani?" My God, my God, why have you forsaken me? It's four words in his native tongue. Two are God's name.

For two thousand years Christians have tried to give answers and explanations for this scene, have tried to explain why things had to be this way. But there are some moments when all answers fail. No explanation will ever turn this scene to sense. No words will ever be enough.

When every word and explanation fails, what is left to us? What remains is Jesus. In Jesus, God made a choice to lend the power of God's own breath to our human cry of confusion and desolation. In Jesus, God made a choice to free-fall with us into darkness.

There may be more answers someday—for Job, for us—answers of the kind we are looking for. A light will someday dawn —a light by which many things will be seen more clearly. But there is also a bright darkness, a weighty silence, an impenetrable mystery that exists at the very center of Christian faith. There is a point at which all words and explanations and answers come apart. A place where all we have said must be unsaid, where all we have known dissolves into unknowing.

But beyond words, beyond silence, beyond questions, beyond explanations, beyond despair, beyond hope, beyond faith, beyond doubt—God remains. To fall into the blackness is to fall into God and find ourselves held there. It's to hear Christ crying with us, in us, for us, and to find even in the deepest, darkest heart of mystery that we are never alone.

36

NATURAL ENEMIES
Living with Uncertainty

There's something seductive about the idea that all the answers you're yearning for are out there somewhere, written in the concrete "print" of the stars or entrails or cards or lines of the palm. In Deuteronomy 18:9-22, God forbids the Israelites from consulting sign readers, fortune-tellers, or diviners. If they want to know what's on God's mind, they're told to talk to their local prophet. You might wonder why a good Israelite would even be tempted to look up a diviner when there's a perfectly legitimate prophet around. Their reasons are probably not so distant from why twenty-first-century people consult astrologers or horoscopes instead of simply showing up at the local pastor's office.

If you ask a Magic 8 Ball whether you should marry Jamie, you get a clear, unambiguous answer: "Without a doubt," or maybe "Run like wildebeests are behind you." The prophet, on the other hand, is more likely to say, "Well, I sense that God is saying that whether this thing between you and Jamie will go well or poorly depends on many things, including the choices you both make along the way to prioritize each other's interests and seek God first and also try budgeting software." (You begin to see why prophetic interactions were not always satisfying.)

Many people I know would probably prefer a Bible that works more like the 8 Ball than a prophet. We'd like our answers to arrive all clear and unambiguous—ideally in short bursts of five words or less. We'd prefer a method of divine messaging that entirely bypasses the risks of human subjectivity, a system of communication from which all prospect of user error has been somehow magically purged. We want a guarantee or a prediction, not a choice; an efficient informational download, not a relationship.

But the shape of the Bible we have suggests that God wants something rather different.

We have a God who chose to be revealed first and foremost through a people. Through a family of ex-slaves, stumbling toward freedom. Through prophets who spoke a word that burned like fire in their bones. Through Jesus and those who followed him and documented what they saw. Through Christians who listened to the Spirit and wrote down what they heard. Through communities that read these documents and confirmed, "Yes, we find God here."

We have a Bible full of unexpected twists and complex pieces that depend, in some significant fashion, on the reader to discern the connections between them. A story that can only be comprehended by those willing to live inside it. Divine communication that must be deciphered through reliance on God's Spirit and each other. Answers that frequently multiply the questions and questions that multiply answers in each new setting in which they're asked.

For some, the tolerance for uncertainty required to navigate such a book feels almost unbearable. With stakes so high, it seems we can hardly afford to get it wrong. Why on earth would God choose to speak in a medium like this?

If God's goal were to produce a people who can negotiate the world with as few missteps as possible, this would indeed seem a very strange means. If a teacher wants her students to pass the exam with the maximum possible right answers, there's one surefire solution: simply share with them the answer key. But there's a reason that (most) teachers don't do this: the goal isn't just to get the answers right. The goal is to actually learn.

It turns out that God's ambition for us is far greater than any ambition we ever had for ourselves. Many of us consider it a good day if we manage to follow a passable percentage of direct orders. But Jesus says, "I don't call you servants any longer, because servants don't know what their master is doing. Instead, I call you friends, because everything I heard from my Father I have made known to you" (John 15:15).

According to Jesus, God's primary aim in relating to humanity is not simply driving up performance scores on standardized tests. If that were the goal, God would be better served by creating robots rather than people—after all, robots execute commands far more reliably, do better math, and (at least for now) are far less likely to get distracted by their phone, forget to turn off the gas, and burn down the house. But according to Jesus, God's primary investment is in relationship, intimacy, even—strange as it sounds—friendship. God is interested in relating to free, creative beings who don't just execute God's orders but actually learn to know God's mind and even grow to share God's core desires.

This is a risky, messy business, because learning always involves mistakes, and relationship always requires a true back-and-forth, a real interplay, a responsiveness from both parties. There is no relationship or growth without vulnerability. But these are risks God has embraced in giving us a Bible like the one we possess, and most of all in the sending of Jesus himself. God has proved willing to take the long way around in order to shape people in the grown-up image of Christ.

Participating in a process like this means living with some level of uncertainty as we learn and grow. But God hasn't simply tossed us into the deep end without a life preserver. For all the ambiguities and questions, the center of the story remains clearly defined. The church has passed down through the centuries not just a book—the Bible—but the interpretive key to unlocking it, what the early Christians called "the rule of faith." This core story of how God has acted to rescue the world through Jesus has been the center of the church's message from the very beginning. It is the anchor that keeps interpretation from being carried too far off course as we seek to be genuinely responsive to the Spirit's movement and not simply driven along by the shifting winds of the times.

There are many things about which the Bible witnesses clearly and consistently: God is gracious, compassionate, and slow to anger. God is a deliverer who cares for the oppressed. God is a jealous God who desires holiness, lives entirely devoted to God and God's purposes. At all times and in all things, God looks like Jesus. On these matters there is no debate or ambiguity in Scripture. These things we can assert with a high level of confidence. The foundation is firm enough to ground life on as we listen and discern the rest.

But for some of us, perhaps, our uncertainty burrows into this very foundation. We are intrigued, perhaps, by the Bible's witness to Jesus' life, death, and resurrection. And yet, facing such a story, it's impossible to feel sure.

The answer to uncertainty is not to refuse to believe anything. The answer to uncertainty is faith, an invitation to leap in the direction of a worthy vision and see where it leads. If we see in the Bible and in Jesus a vision of God and human existence that seems so good and beautiful we long for it to be true, that's enough to get started. We simply wade into the story, practice the strokes, and watch to see what happens.

The true enemy of biblical faith is not uncertainty. It is not doubt. It's not being wrong on occasion. Uncertainty is faith confirming itself through experience. Doubt is faith keeping its eyes open. Being wrong is part of the journey of learning. Faith has only one natural predator: fear.

When it comes to reading the Bible, discerning the Spirit, knowing God, nothing is more toxic than fear. Many of us have learned to live with a whole lot of fear. We fear angering God. We fear our opponent winning the argument. We fear taking a stand. We fear risking our lives on something we're not sure about. We fear the church coming off the tracks. We fear the world falling to pieces. We fear losing our faith. We fear discovering we were wrong about the whole thing all along.

The trouble with fear is it has a nasty habit of holding on so tightly that it strangles to death the very things it set out to protect. Fear works like a constant droning in our ears that drowns out any other voice, including God's. It keeps us lying on our mat even after we've been healed, never getting up to try our new leaping legs. Fear is a black hole that consumes all life and truth in its path.

But the Bible itself speaks a clear word back to fear.

First, it says, God is on the throne. The outcome of history is not determined by us and doesn't depend on us alone. We can't derail God's story by making mistakes along the way. The Spirit of Truth is stronger and more persistent than the spirit of human error. In the end, Christ's kingdom will still come, and God will have God's way regardless.

Second, we are covered by an abundant grace that is enough for all of us. Jesus died to place a claim on us that simply can't be broken. We can't flunk out of this story by messing up too many times, and neither can our neighbors. We can listen, learn, redirect, and grow; we can dare to love and truly live, with the confidence of people who know their destiny is already written in the victory of Christ.

Third, one of the most consistent commands, issued dozens of times in the Bible, is that we seek. But the Bible does not command the act of finding. The author of Hebrews writes, "It is impossible to please God without faith because the one who draws near to God must believe that he exists and that he rewards people who try to find him" (Hebrews 11:6). The operative word here is *try*. The task of seeking God with all the strength and tools we possess—this is our central directive. But the outcome, the results of that dogged pursuit—that is entirely on God. It is God who must give God's self to be known. More than that, the good news of Jesus is anchored in the assurance that we are being found, even despite ourselves. God is the ultimate Finder.

There's a new level of freedom when we realize these things. We don't have to live every day and enter every conversation with the fear that everything is about to come apart. We can dare to get on with the real business of life: loving God with everything we have and are and loving our neighbors as ourselves—by Jesus' own account, the very heart of the Bible's call.

What can we really be sure of? Our desire for God is only a small echo of God's desire for us. Where we seek truly and fully, God will show up to meet us. We may not see or hear or interpret God perfectly, but God will be there either way, finding us time and time again. And in all that we don't know, Who we do know is enough.

CONCLUSION

In Genesis 32 a man named Jacob, perhaps best remembered for his habit of screwing over family members to get what he wants, is camped out on the banks of the Jabbok River. For the first time in two decades he's going to meet with the brother whose inheritance he stole. Jacob is lying under the stars—wondering how angry his twin still is and whether his biceps are as huge and hairy as he remembers and jumping at small noises—when he sees a shadow moving in the dark.

Jacob reacts from pure instinct. He launches himself at the shadow and tumbles head over heels with it into the sand. He's got his arm wrapped around the shadow's thigh, his knee locked around its neck. He is on this guy with the frenzy of a rabid raccoon. There's grunting and hair flying and a little high-pitched squealing. Fast-forward a few hours and they're still there, tangled up together, both sweating and wheezing and covered in grit, but refusing to let go.

It's only as the sun begins to creep over the horizon that it starts to dawn on Jacob: this body beneath him isn't as hairy as the brother he remembers. Nor does it feel like his wiry old uncle Laban, whom he also recently cheated, come to wring his thieving neck. For the first time it occurs to Jacob that he might not know who he's wrestling with.

Jacob's thigh muscle has been torn in the scuffle, and the stranger suggests it might be time to just call it a day. But Jacob stubbornly refuses to loosen his grip. He declares, "No way! I'll never let you go until you bless me!" Even now, after being up all night and with his leg screaming in pain, Jacob is absolutely determined to get his money's worth, to get whatever it is this stranger might have to give him.

The stranger finally decides it's the right time for introductions. "What's your name?" he asks Jacob. When Jacob replies, the stranger says, "Starting today you'll have a new name. Your name is Israel (which means 'one who struggles with God'), because you have wrestled with God and with people and have overcome."

At this statement, the fine hairs stand up on Jacob's neck, and he finally asks the all-important question. Or it would have been a question, but because he's Jacob, it comes out more like a demand: "Tell me your name." The stranger offers no answer except the cryptic reply, "Why are you asking me that?" But the stranger does reach out and give Jacob the blessing he was looking for. And as the sun comes up, Jacob limps back to his friends slightly dazed and awed, whispering over and over to himself, "I have seen *God*, face-to-face . . ."

This strange little story is my favorite in the entire Bible. Something about the encounter between Jacob and the stranger reminds me very much of what it's like to relate to Scripture. To truly engage with the Bible honestly is to enter a wrestling match. We struggle to get our arms (and our heads) around it. We grapple with it through the night. We try to pin it down.

When we finally discover that it is beyond us, two choices remain. We can give it up, decide it's not worth the struggle, and walk away. Or we can wrap ourselves around its ankle like a boa constrictor and simply refuse to let go.

Sooner or later, almost every reader of the Bible I've ever met begins to feel the longing Jacob feels for an identifying name. We want a term that will sum up this mysterious force we're clinging to and grappling with to the point of exhaustion. We want to know What. This. Thing. Is.

But the Bible declines to give us its name, just as the stranger declines to give his name to Jacob. It refuses to be reduced to a bite-sized definition that we can control. It is not a prize that can be somehow possessed. It can only be encountered, never mastered. It simply is what it is, a living force that in the end always retains its freedom.

But to lack a "master name" or "master term" to sum up the Bible and its nature does not mean the struggle itself is without substantial meaning. Jacob never receives a name for the one with whom he wrestles, but in the end, he himself is named by the act of wrestling. And this is the heart of the matter. What we say about the Bible is far less defining than what the Bible says about us. We are the ones reshaped, renamed by our encounter with it. We are the ones formed and defined by the struggle. In all our efforts to capture and contain, we are the ones captured and transformed.

I suspect it is no coincidence that Jacob walks away from his encounter limping. Anyone who grapples seriously with Scripture can expect to limp a little. I have been immensely blessed by the Bible—healed, freed, challenged, unsettled, carried into the very presence of God. But that blessing has come with a limp I will carry all my life—the wounding of unresolved questions and painful experience that is never quite fully answered in the way I hope. Many others can say the same.

But that's okay. Such limps remind us that no one, however strong, is as all-knowing as God. They make us humble in our boasts. They simultaneously mark an honorable struggle and bespeak our limits. They insure against the reduction of genuine God-encounter to mere idol-talk.

What we cannot master, label, or systematize can still profoundly change us. Such is the power of the Bible. We are changed by the very act of simply grappling with it. As we struggle with the Bible, we are strengthened—in Christ-shaped imagination, in capacity for faithful action. More than that, when we wrestle with the Bible, we begin to feel beneath our hands the very contours of God. Even without a name, we learn real recognition—the scent of God's nearness, the sound of God's heartbeat, the feel of God's breath.

Like Jacob, we may greet the dawn with no clearer name for the one with whom we've struggled. Yet we may still declare in awe that somehow, in the process of wrestling, we have glimpsed the face of God.

ACKNOWLEDGMENTS

A project of this scope would not be conceivable without the years spent studying under many fine scholars and teachers of the Bible. I am grateful for every one of these professors, who somehow kept the Word always fresh and new for me. I owe a particular debt of gratitude to some whose distinctive passions and insights continue to shape how I myself read and teach sacred Scripture: Michael Gorman, Douglas Campbell, James Crenshaw, Richard Hays, Paul Borgman, Marvin Wilson, Elaine Phillips, Kavin Rowe, David Mathewson, Jo Bailey Wells, and Stanley Hauerwas. While vastly different in their perspectives, each one teaches in such a way as to leave their students dazzled by the beauty of the Bible and even more by the God who shines through it. Many of their insights are reflected in this book. Any errors it possesses are mine, and where we simply understand differently what we see in Scripture, I continue to rejoice in our common allegiance to our one Lord, Jesus Christ.

My oral defense team at Portland Seminary (at George Fox University) provided helpful feedback during the early stages of the drafting process—Nijay Gupta, Jami Noling-

Auth, Leonard Sweet, and Dottie Escobedo-Frank. I'm also grateful for my editor, Valerie Weaver-Zercher, and the team at Herald Press for making this project possible at exactly the right time.

In the many classes I conducted throughout the years on how to read the Bible, my own congregations at Trinity Mennonite Church and Albany Mennonite Church asked wonderful, difficult questions that forced me to wrestle in new ways with my own convictions around Scripture. I'm so deeply thankful for their honesty, openness, and patience with me as I have stumbled and grown. My colleagues at Trinity have brought joy to my life through the last few years of intensive research and writing, and I feel blessed to be partnering with them in the work of the gospel. I'm especially grateful to Scott Peterson, whose incisive feedback and insightful questions are nearly always frighteningly on target and who consistently sees what lies in my blind spots.

Above all, I'm thankful for my parents, to whom this book is dedicated, who first taught me the songs and stories of the Bible and whose passion for God and for people was critical in igniting my own.

NOTES

Introduction

1 For helpful examinations of the early church's approach to Scripture, its nature, and its purpose, see Justin S. Holcomb, ed., *Christian Theologies of Scripture: A Comparative Introduction* (New York: New York University Press, 2006); and Michael Graves, *The Inspiration and Interpretation of Scripture: What the Early Church Can Teach Us* (Grand Rapids, MI: Eerdmans, 2014).

Chapter 1

1 For a compelling argument regarding the personal, intuitive dimension of scientific knowledge, see Michael Polanyi, *Personal Knowledge: Toward a Post-Critical Philosophy* (Chicago: University of Chicago Press, 1962).

Chapter 3

1 For another take on why our understanding of the nature of the Bible should be shifted away from the paradigm of the instruction manual, see Peter Enns, *The Bible Tells Me So: Why Defending Scripture Has Made Us Unable to Read It* (New York: HarperOne, 2014).

Chapter 5

1 For a more detailed description of this process, see Walter J. Ong, *Orality and Literacy: The Technologizing of the Word* (London: Routledge, 1991).

2 Craig D. Allert, *A High View of Scripture? The Authority of the*

Bible and the Formation of the New Testament Canon (Grand Rapids, MI: Baker Academic, 2007), 155.

Chapter 6
1   For an in-depth examination of the process by which the canon came together, see F. F. Bruce, *The Canon of Scripture* (Downers Grove, IL: InterVarsity Press, 1988).
2   Craig D. Allert, *A High View of Scripture? The Authority of the Bible and the Formation of the New Testament Canon* (Grand Rapids, MI: Baker Academic, 2007), 65.

Chapter 8
1   For a more thorough introduction to the entire Christian story than I can provide here, I recommend Bruxy Cavey, *Reunion: The Good News of Jesus for Seekers, Saints, and Sinners* (Harrisonburg, VA: Herald Press, 2017).
2   The idea of the image of God as meaning "authorized representative" is convincingly argued by J. Richard Middleton in *The Liberating Image: The Imago Dei in Genesis 1* (Grand Rapids, MI: Brazos Press, 2005).

Chapter 10
1   This term originated in the writings of Paul Ricoeur. See Paul Ricoeur, *Freud and Philosophy: An Essay on Interpretation* (New Haven: Yale University Press, 1970).
2   For a helpful discussion of the current academic preoccupation with critique-centered readings, see Rita Felski, *The Limits of Critique* (Chicago: University of Chicago Press, 2015).

Storytime: Unwrapping the Book of Jonah
1   For a philosophical exploration of the rationality of believing in miracles, I again commend Michael Polanyi, *Personal Knowledge: Toward a Post-Critical Philosophy* (Chicago: University of Chicago Press, 1962).

Chapter 11
1   Nathan Hatch presents a highly relevant discussion of the impact of democratic populism on systems that rely for validation on

any sort of specialized knowledge or authority. See Nathan Hatch, *The Democratization of American Christianity* (New Haven: Yale University Press, 1989).

2   See Alister E. McGrath, *The Intellectual Origins of the European Reformation*, 2nd ed. (Malden, MA: Blackwell, 2004).

3   For further introduction to the role and necessity of interpretation, I recommend Scot McKnight, *The Blue Parakeet: Rethinking How You Read the Bible* (Grand Rapids, MI: Zondervan, 2008).

Chapter 12

1   Example noted by Joseph McGlynn III and Matthew S. Mc-Glone, "Language," in *Encyclopedia of Deception*, ed. Timothy R. Levine (Thousand Oaks, CA: Sage, 2014), 584.

2   To explore the transformative effect of reading literary context, I recommend the translation work of Robert Alter, who reads Old Testament texts with a sharp eye to literary context and detail. See as one example Robert Alter, *The David Story* (New York: W. W. Norton, 1999).

Chapter 13

1   Kenneth E. Bailey, *Jesus through Middle Eastern Eyes: Cultural Studies in the Gospels* (Downers Grove, IL: IVP Academic, 2008), 29–33.

2   For a more detailed exploration of historical background relevant to the Bible's statements on women, see John Temple Bristow, *What Paul Really Said about Women* (New York: HarperCollins, 1988).

3   If you're looking for a study Bible to try out, I have several recommendations. *The NIV Cultural Backgrounds Study Bible* (Zondervan, 2016) includes pictures and charts in addition to the usual study notes. *The CEB Study Bible* (Common English Bible, 2013) is somewhat more limited in the sheer quantity of information provided but is composed by a strong team of biblical scholars from diverse Christian traditions. *The Harper Collins Study Bible* (HarperOne, 2006) is commonly used by college and graduate-level biblical studies programs.

Chapter 15

1   I am indebted for this insight to Paul Borgman, *David, Saul, and God: Rediscovering an Ancient Story* (New York: Oxford University

Press, 2008), 18–19. For another example of the kind of insight that a close narrative reading can produce, see Paul Borgman, *The Way according to Luke: Hearing the Whole Story of Luke-Acts* (Grand Rapids, MI: Eerdmans, 2006).

Chapter 16

1   Robert Frost, "The Road Not Taken," in *Mountain Interval* (New York: Henry Holt, 1916).

2   William Shakespeare, Sonnet 18, lines 1–2.

3   My understanding of the function of the cursing psalms has been greatly aided by the work of Ellen Davis. See Ellen Davis, *Getting Involved with God: Rediscovering the Old Testament* (Cambridge: Cowley, 2001), 26–29.

Chapter 17

1   Walter Brueggemann offers an excellent introduction to the broad framework of relationship between God and Israel, of which the Law is one part. See Walter Brueggemann, *An Unsettling God: The Heart of the Hebrew Bible* (Minneapolis: Fortress Press, 2009).

Chapter 18

1   To explore further the distinctive call and character of the prophet, I recommend Abraham J. Heschel, *The Prophets* (Peabody, MA: Prince Press, 2004).

Chapter 19

1   The status of Song of Songs among the wisdom literature of the Bible is disputed by some scholars, who argue that the book lacks some of the defining characteristics of the genre and should therefore be understood as fundamentally unique within the biblical canon. Parts of the book of Psalms (such as Psalm 49 and 73) are also often classified among the Bible's wisdom literature.

2   Ariel Bloch and Chana Bloch offer a truly lovely translation of Songs of Songs, complete with detailed translation notes. Ariel Bloch and Chana Bloch, *The Song of Songs: A New Translation* (Berkeley: University of California Press, 1995).

Chapter 20

1 For an insightful examination of how the four gospel writers each portray the truth of Jesus' divine identity in relationship to their own Old Testament Scriptures, I highly recommend Richard Hays, *Reading Backwards: Figural Christology and Fourfold Gospel Witness* (Waco, TX: Baylor University Press, 2014).

Chapter 21

1 I was first introduced to improvisation as a metaphor for the Christian life by my former pastor Samuel Wells. See Samuel Wells, *Improvisation: The Drama of Christian Ethics* (Grand Rapids, MI: Brazos Press, 2004).

2 A perfect example of the impact of headings may be found in the 1984 edition of the NIV, which places a heading break between Ephesians 5:21 and 22. This heading location represents an interpretive decision to separate Paul's appeal for mutual submission from his instruction for submission of wives. The 2015 edition of the NIV relocates the heading to before 5:21, so that the appeal for mutual submission and the instruction to wives are now read together as one piece. The potential interpretive impact is substantial, affecting whether the submission of wives should be read as something unique to their role as women or merely as a particular reiteration of an instruction that applies to men and women both. In this case, the location of the heading may significantly influence how you envision the ideal for Christian marriage.

Chapter 22

1 For further guidance on how to interpret the wealth of symbols and theme of Revelation, I recommend Michael Reddish's Smyth and Helwys Bible Commentary, *Revelation* (Macon, GA: Smyth and Helwys, 2001). For an example of a rich reading of Revelation that attends both to its original historical context and to its extraordinary contemporary relevance, I recommend Eugene Peterson, *Reversed Thunder: The Revelation of John and the Praying Imagination* (New York: HarperOne, 1988).

2 I owe credit for this analogy between Revelation and visual art to Michael Gorman, whose 2008 class at Duke Divinity School on the book of Revelation emphasized artistic representation of Revelation's message and had a major impact on my own reading.

Chapter 23

1   Benjamin D. Sommer, "Introduction: Scriptures in Jewish Tradition and Traditions as Jewish Scripture," in *Jewish Concepts of Scripture: A Comparative Introduction*, ed. Benjamin D. Sommer (New York: New York University Press, 2012), 4, EBSCOhost.

Chapter 24

1   While Jesus himself does not directly address the sacrificial system, the book of Hebrews explores how Jesus reveals the true meaning to which the sacrificial system pointed—God's willingness to take on God's self the consequences of our failings. The sacrificial procedures required by the Law are deemed no longer necessary, as their ultimate purpose has been fulfilled in the death of Christ.

Chapter 26

1   For another take on the relationship between the cross of Jesus and Old Testament violence, check out Gregory A. Boyd, *Cross Vision: How the Crucifixion of Jesus Makes Sense of Old Testament Violence* (Minneapolis: Fortress Press, 2017).

Storytime: Unwrapping Genesis 6:5–9:29

1   While I have emphasized the ordinary, even deeply flawed, character of Abraham as portrayed within the Genesis story, it is worth noting that from the perspective of the biblical canon as a whole, Abraham turns out to be arguably one of the most remarkable individuals who ever lived (see Romans 4 and Hebrews 11). My point here, however, is to observe that unlike the personal accolades given Noah from the very start of his story, Abraham's exceptional qualities emerge only gradually as he journeys together with God, making many mistakes along the way. And while Noah is known for his personal blamelessness, both the Old and the New Testaments suggest that Abraham's defining, exceptional quality is simply his extraordinary trust in God. In other words, if the story implies that Noah was remarkable for who he was, Abraham was remarkable for whom he trusted.

Chapter 27

1   My thanks to Eric Shenk for first suggesting this metaphor.

2   I've been particularly influenced in my thinking about transformational reading by the work of M. Robert Mulholland Jr., who has expanded the traditional four-step Benedictine practice of *lectio divina* ("divine reading") into six steps and suggested a place for the tools of study within it. It should be noted, however, that in its purest form, *lectio divina* bypasses more analytical notions of study to encourage a direct encounter with God through the text. In this sense both the practice Mulholland describes and my own remix of it should probably be understood as something distinct from *lectio divina*. See M. Robert Mulholland Jr., *Invitation to a Journey: A Road Map for Spiritual Formation*, rev. ed. (Downers Grove, IL: InterVarsity Press, 2016), 129–33.

Chapter 28

1   What Jesus actually said was "When they force you to go one mile, go with them two." The likely history of this command to go "the extra mile" involved a practice by which a Roman military person could forcibly conscript a passing civilian to carry a load for up to one Roman mile. Jesus gave this instruction at a time when Israel was under Roman oppression.

Chapter 31

1   I've been enriched a great deal in my own understanding of the relationship between Scripture and Spirit by new scholarship developing within the Pentecostal tradition. I believe these scholars are beginning to direct attention to critical aspects of biblical discernment that have been severely underrepresented in the hermeneutical debates of both evangelical and mainline Protestants. I recommend as a starting place *Pentecostal Hermeneutics: A Reader*, ed. Lee Roy Martin (Leiden: Brill, 2013). John Christopher Thomas's contribution to this book, a chapter entitled "Women, Pentecostalism, and the Bible: An Experiment in Pentecostal Hermeneutics," is particularly notable in its observations about the significance of Acts 15.

Chapter 32

1   The best description I've heard of the relationship between the Bible and the Spirit's activity in the ongoing Christian life comes

from the work of N. T. Wright. See N. T. Wright, "How Can the Bible Be Authoritative?" *Vox Evangelica* 21 (1991): 7–32. Text available at http://ntwrightpage.com/Wright_Bible_Authoritative.htm.

Chapter 33

1 This authority is first delegated to Peter as representative of the Christian community in Matthew 16:19 and then extended to the church as a whole in Matthew 18:18. M. Eugene Boring, *The Gospel of Matthew*, New Interpreter's Bible Commentary (Nashville: Abingdon Press, 1994), 346.

2 Thank you to Dr. Leonard Sweet for that striking observation.

3 For a provocative exploration of the impact of community on reading, see Tim Conder and Daniel Rhodes, *Free for All: Rediscovering the Bible in Community* (Grand Rapids, MI: Baker Books, 2009).

Chapter 35

1 Moshe Halbertal, *People of the Book: Canon, Meaning, and Authority* (Cambridge, MA: Harvard University Press, 2009), 50–51, ProQuest.

2 As the ancient Christian thinker Augustine once rather sharply put it in a discussion about the interpretation of Genesis, "See how stupid it is, among so large a mass of entirely correct interpretations which can be elicited from these words, rashly to assert that a particular one has best claim to be Moses' view, and by destructive disputes to offend against charity itself, which is the principle of everything he said in the texts we are attempting to expound." Augustine, *Confessions* XII 25.35.

THE AUTHOR

Meghan Larissa Good is teaching pastor at Trinity Mennonite Church in Glendale, Arizona. She has degrees from Gordon College, Duke Divinity School, and Portland Seminary. In addition to being a passionate preacher and storyteller, Good is in demand as a speaker on hermeneutics, Anabaptism, and millennials and the church.